# Geography of Jammu and Kashmir

*This book is dedicated to*
*Late Manzoor Ahmad who was a staunch believer of 'Almighty' and whose love and affection always inspired me in my academic pursuits and life.*

# Geography of Jammu and Kashmir

Majid Husain

RAJESH PUBLICATIONS
NEW DELHI - 110002

# Geography of Jammu and Kashmir

*Published by :*
Sanjay Gupta
**RAJESH PUBLICATIONS**
1, Ansari Road, Darya Ganj New Delhi - 110002
Email : rajeshpublications@gmail.com
rajeshpubdelhi@gmail.com
Website : www.rajeshpublications.com



First Edition : 1987
Second Edition : 1998
Third Edition (Revised) : 2002
Fourth Edition (Revised & Enlarged) : 2005
Fifth Edition : 2006
Reprint : 2024

ISBN: 978-81-85891-16-3

*Printed at :*
AM Printing Press
Delhi-110096

*The University of Kashmir*

UNIVERSITY CAMPUS
HAZRATBAL
SRINAGAR-6

June 3, 1986

VICE-CHANCELLOR

# Foreword

The State of Jammu and Kashmir is a fascinating geographic region including a unique blend of natural and cultural characterisitcs. There are very few systematic and faithful accounts of this state. Prof. Majid Husain's book on 'Geography of Jammu and Kashmir' fills this vital gap and provides valuable information and analysis on the physical, economic and social aspects. In this book the author reveals a rare understanding of the physiographic and socio economic setting of the state and presents a rational account which is marked for vividness and clarity. The whole book is written in a simple style which even an undergraduate will find easy to understand and comprehend. I do hope that the lead given by Prof. Majid Husain will be followed by other geographers and we shall soon have a series of works on the geographical characteristics of the State of Jammu & Kashmir.

**Prof. S. Manzoor Alam**

# Preface

The present work 'Geography of Jammu & Kashmir' provides a systematic account of the northern-most state of the country which has great diversity in its physiography, ethno-cultural milieu, economy and over-all geographical personality. The work incorporated three sections, namely, (i) physical setting, (ii) social personality and (iii) economy of the state.

Part First of the book opens with a brief discussion on the geological history, physiographic features and major drainage systems of the state. Chapter Second gives a precise account of the prevailing weather and climatic conditions and their impact on the agricultural operations, cropping patterns and occupations of the people of Jammu, Kashmir and Ladakh Divisions. The flora and fauna and major soil groups have been discussed in Chapter Third, while Chapter Fourth deals with the minerals resource base of the state, their spatial distribution and utilization.

The social personality of the state discussed in Part II of the book includes chapters on peopling, major ethnic groups, transhumance, growth pattern of population, demographic attributes, urban centres and the process of urbanization.

The last part of the book gives an insight into the economy of the State and occupational structure of the people. The agricultural systems, industries, tourism, transport and trade of the state have been described systematically in this section.

The book written in an easy and cogent style, it is hoped,

will be of immense help for the teachers and students of geography as well as for the general readers who are interested in the habitat, economy and society of the Jammu and Kashmir state.

In a work of this nature an author must rely extensively upon material already published and the present work is no exception. List of material consulted by the author, which might with profit be studied by the reader, are given at the end of each chapter. The author expresses his sincere thanks to all those scholars whose works have been consulted in the preparation of the present book.

Prof. S. Manzoor Alam, Vice-Chancellor, University of Kashmir, Srinagar, inspired the author for writing a systematic geographical account of the Jammu and Kashmir State for which he feels highly indebted. The initial plan of the book was discussed with Prof. C.D. Deshpande during his stay in the Department of Geography and Regional Development, University of Kashmir in 1985, who gave valuable suggestions about the framework of study. For all his guidance I must express my sincere gratitudes to late Prof. C.D. Deshpande.

The cartography of maps and diagrams was done by Ms. Ghadir Fatima and Mr. Khurshid Anwar, Dept. of Geography & Regional Development for which the author expresses his sincere thanks. Thanks are also due to Mr. A.M. Wani, Mr. Mukhtar Ahmad, Dr. S. Ajaz Faried and Dr. Shamim A. Shah for their assistance in the form of photographic work. The author is also indebted to his colleagues and students and Dr. Mohammed Aslam Islahi, Professor Dept. of Arabic, who provided a congenial atmosphere to complete the work in record time.

My thanks are also due to my family members, especially to my wife, whose patience has made possible the labour necessary in the preparation of this work. Grateful mentions should be made of Mr. Javed Alam, Dr. Shagufta Bano Husain, Mr. A. Rahman and Mrs. Shahida Naz and Mrs. Saifi Zaka, Mr. Mansoor Majid whose diligence in their studies inspired me to concentrate on the task seriously. The smiling faces of M.A. Rahman, Madeeha Javed, Jibraan Mansoor, R.A. Rahman, Fareeha Javed and Areeb Mansoor were a great source of strength for the author for which I thank them and pray to God for their long and enjoyable life.

Mr. Mohammad Siddique Dar, University of Kashmir also deserves thanks who typed much of the manuscript efficiently. **Mr. M.L. Gupta, Publisher, Rajesh Publications, Darya Ganj, New Delhi-110002** took the task with a sense of commitment and dedication which were crucial in the publication of the book in record time. The author expresses his gratitude to the publisher and his designer for the jacket cover of the book.

In spite of valuable suggestions from learned scholars, there are imperfections. In order to overcome the shortcomings of the present volume, comments from teachers, students and experts will be welcomed so that the subsequent editions may be improved.

**Majid Husain**

# Note on the Revised Edition

Looking at the popularity of the First and Second editions of the 'Geography of Jammu and Kashmir' the book has been revised in which most of the suggestions given by the eminent scholars, teachers and students have been incorporated. In fact, the third edition is an attempt to remove the shortcomings and weaknesses of the first and second editions.

Apart from updating and improving the contents and the text of the book, the latest available data (2001), statistics and information have been computed, tabulated and analysed in the revised edition. Attempt has also been made to give a comprehensive bibliography on the physical personality and cultural landscape of the state. It is hoped that the revised edition will fulfill the needs of the under-graduate and post-graduate students of geography alike, and shall work as reference book for those who are interested in the physical diversity and economic disparities of the State of Jammu and Kashmir. The volume will also be of immense help for those who are interested in the planning and development of the state and shall motivate them to learn more and probe further about this unique and one of the most beautiful states of India often been called as '*Paradise on Earth*'.

March, 2005

**Dr. Majid Husain**
109, Zakir Bagh
New Delhi-110025

# Contents

# List of Figures

# List of Tables

# List of Plates

PART - I

# PHYSICAL SETTING

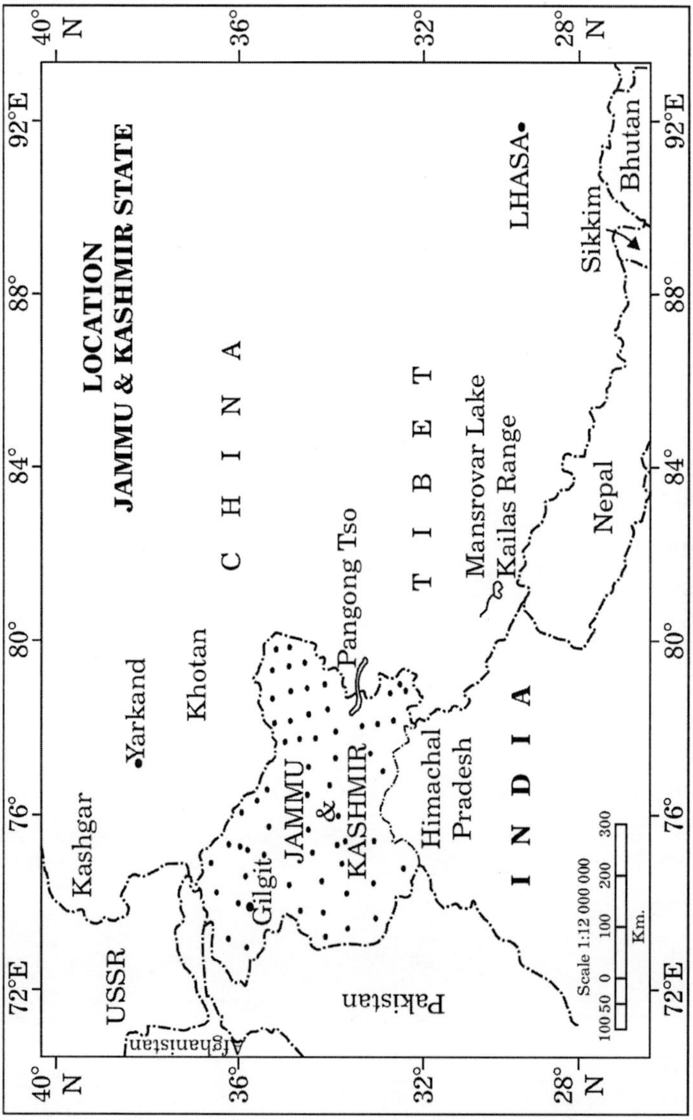


**Fig. 1 : Based Upon Survey of India Map**

Chapter-I

# Geology and Relief

The state of Jammu and Kashmir - a symbol of national integration and unity has a unique geographical personality. It is well endowed in renewable-natural resources. Its mighty rivers, evergreen forest, snow covered peaks, invigorating climate and human population are unparallel in the world. It stretches between 32°17'N to 37°6'N latitudes and 73°26'E to 80°30'E longitudes (Fig. 1).

The state of Jammu and Kashmir comprising the divisions of Ladakh, Jammu and Kashmir has an area of 2.22 lakh sq. km. including those parts which are under the occupation of Pakistan and China. According to the census of 2001, its population was about 10.14 millions. The average density of population in 1981 was 59 persons per sq. km. which went upto 100 in 2001. It is bounded by Tibet in the east, China and Afghanistan in the north and Pakistan in the west, while the southern and south-eastern boundaries are made by the Punjab and Himachal-Pradesh states of India.

## Geology

The state of Jammu and Kashmir carries one of the finest developed sequence of rocks right from the Archaen Era to the Recent Age. The spatial distribution of rocks of different geological periods has been described chronologically in the following paras.

### Archean

The Oldest rocks of the earth crust are Archean which are also known as the Precambrian, but sometimes used to older Precambrian rocks. The Archean rocks (locally called as Salkhala Series) include granites, gneisses and schists. These rocks are found in the north-western parts of the Kashmir Valley (Karnah District), Nanga Parbat, Zanskar and Ladakh. These rocks are also found in the southern parts of Pir-Panjal in the vicinity of Ramban, Kishtwar and Bhadarwah.

### Palaeozoic (Dravidian Group)

The Palaeozoic rocks are extensively developed in the State of Jammu and Kashmir. The Palaeozoic rocks are divisible into the Silurian, Devonian, Carboniferous and Permian Systems.

The Silurian rocks consisting of sandy shales, shale, sandstone, and yellow-limestone are found near Aishmuqam and parts of Lidder Valley in Anantnag District.

The Devonian rocks lie conformably over the Silurian rocks on both flanks of Lidder as thick beds of quarzite, known as Muth quartzites, Rocks of this age are also found on the southern flanks of Pir-Panjal.

Carboniferous System named from the widespread occurrence of carbon in the form of coal in these rocks. The carboniferous rocks lie conformably over the Muth-quartzites of Devonian Age in Aishmuqam, Kotsu. Panjal-Range, Zanskar-Range and Banihar Valley.

The upper system of Palaeozoic is known as Permian. The Permian rocks are composed of shale, dark arnacious-shales and limestone. These formations are found in Pir-Panjal, Upper Singh, Lidder Valley (Kashmir Division) and Katra to Poonch in Jammu Division.

### Mesozoic-Era

The period of 'middle life' comprises of Triassic, Jurassic

and Cretaceous Systems. The Mesozoic was preceded by the Palaeozoic and followed by the Cainozoic Eras. The most spectacular elements of Mesozoic faunas were the giant reptiles.

The Triassic formations are found in the Sindh Valley, Lidder Valley and northern slopes of Pir-Panjal Range.

The Jurassic System is named from the Jura Mountains of France. The fauna of Jurassic was extremely diverse and varied. The dominant terrestrial animals were the dinosaurs, which reached their maximum size in the Jurassic and occupied most of the ecological niches. The flora of the Jurassic included many forms still living at the present day such as conifers and ferns. The Jurassic formation is found in the Valley of Banihal.

The Cretaceous System has been derived from the Greek word 'Creta' means 'chalk'. During this period there had been a wide spread of marine transgression. The rock formation of this period are found in Astor, Burzil, Dras and Ladakh.

### Cainozoic Era

The Cainozoic Era suceeds Mesozoic and ends at the Quaternary Period. It is commonly used as a synonym of Tertiary. It comprises of the Eocene and Recent Pleistocene Systems. The Karewa uplands bordering the Valley of Kashmir and river terraces of Jhelum, Chenab and Ravi came into existence during the Eocene Period. The new alluviums of these rivers fall in the Recent Period of Cainozoic Era.

### Geomorphic Features

Morphologically, the state is divisible into three distinct regions i.e. Jammu, Kashmir and Ladakh. Each of the three regions has distinct physiographic features. Nevertheless the administrative boundaries do not conform to the physiographic boundaries. On the basis of physiography the state is divisible into –

(i) The Outer-Plains

(ii) The Siwaliks
(iii) The Middle Himalayas
(iv) The Valley of Kashmir
(v) The Greater Himalayas
(vi) The Plateau of Ladakh

## The Outer Plains (Andareah and Bajwat)

The state of Jammu and Kashmir in the south is rimmed by an alluvial plain of the Chenab, Tawi and Ravi rivers and their tributaries. In width it varies from seven to thirty kilometres. It sprawls in the southern parts of Akhnoor, Ranbirsinghpura, (R.S. Pura), Samba and Kathua. This Plain constitutes a part of the Great Plains of India and resembles to the landscape of Punjab. The height of this highly productive plain varies between 325 to 350 metres.

Being in the south of the Siwalik, the Outer Plain of the Jammu Division is traverssed by the namerous hill torrents locally called as *Khads*. These torrents remain dry over the greater parts of the winter and summer seasons and attain enormous size during rains. At the occurrence of rains, the ravines achieve the shape of gushing torrents and its becomes difficult to ford them. Occasionally, at the occurrence of floods these torrents transport massive quantities of sand, red silt, pebbles and shingles. The channels of these torrents are characterised by clumps of reed growth locally called as *Khar*.

The Outer Plains of Jammu are highly fertile and the temperatures permit the cultivation of crops throughout the year. In tracts like Ranbirsinghapura which have been provided with adequate canal and tube-well irrigation, two staple (rice and wheat) and a fodder crop are grown in a year. It is this part of the state in which High Yielding Varieties (HYV) of wheat and rice have been diffused successfully and where the Green Revolution is a big success.

## The Siwaliks

To the north of the Jammu Plains for a distance of about

200 Kms. between Ravi and Jhelum rivers stretch the youngest mountains of the Sub-continent, i.e. the Siwaliks. The width of the Siwaliks is between 20 to 50 kms. and height between 600 to 1220 metres above the sea level in the state of Jammu and Kashmir.

The slopes of Siwaliks facing the outer plains are gentle covered with deciduous forests, evergreen bushes and numerous scrubs. The northern slopes have steep slopes with thin cover of vegetation. In the Siwaliks to the east of Jammu city are situated the Mansar and Saruinsar lakes at an elevation of about 600 metres.

The undulating slopes, adjacent to the plains upto an elevation of 300 metres between Ravi and Chenab rivers are locally known as *Kandi*. The *Kandi* land is characterised by numerous torrents, dissected soils and scarcity of water. Consequently, agriculture in *Kandi* areas is exclusively dependent on rains. The rate of soil erosion during rainy season is heavy. The people (Gujjars) practice cattle keeping mixed with maize, pulses and oilseeds cultivation. Economically, this is the most underdeveloped part of the state in which the Gujjars and Paharis are living at a poor level of subsistence.

The second largest city of the state and the winter capital Jammu is situated at an altitude of 366 metres above the sea level on the southern slope of the Siwaliks along the banks of Tawi river.

In between the Siwaliks and the Lesser Himalayas lie the longitudinal valleys locally known as *Doons/Duns*. The important *Doons* are Basoli, Ramkote, Dansal, Udhampur and Sundarbani. These fertile valleys have a high concentration of population.

### The Middle Himalayas

The Middle Himalayas locally known as *Pahar* (mountain) in Jammu Division sprawl between the Ravi in the east and the Poonch in the west, though they continue towards north-west beyond Muzaffarabad. In elevation they vary between 1820m. to 2240m. The Middle Himalayas have a width of about 60 kilometres in the eastern parts of Jammu Division which decreases to only about 10 kilometres near Rajouri.

The Middle Himalayas in general have an east-west extension. From the ridge, however, a number of side ridges and spurs radiate in all directions. At Tanger, a branch ridge runs due south-west. It is the Trikuta Mountain which have limestone strata. The sacred cave of *Vaishno Devi* is situated in a peak of Trikuta Mountain.

Several important rivers e.g. Tawi, Manawar-Tawi, Basantar and Ujh have their sources in the Middle Himalayas. The rock strata of Middle Himalayas is dominated by sandstone, shale and light-yellow limestone of Miocene Murree System.

The southern slopes of Middle Himalayas are covered by forest. In the high altitudinal zones *deodar* (oak), blue-pine and silve-fir dominate, while in the areas of low heights i.e. below 1800 meters, the monsoon deciduous forest and scrubs constitute the dominant species.

The Jammu-Srinagar National Highway No. 1, has been carved out through the Middle Himalayas which crosses this system at Patni-Top Pass at an altitude of about 1950 metres.

Excepting the river terraces and river-valleys, cultivation of crops is not an important economic activity in the Middle Himalayas. The people are largely dependent on forestry lumbering, herding, cattle keeping and tourist industry for their sustenance.

## The Valley of Kashmir

The Valley of Kashmir often been termed as '*the paradise on earth*' is famous for its lakes, clear streams, green turf, magnificent trees, mighty mountains, cool air sweet-water and highly productive soils, growing paddy, maize, apples, almonds, walnut and saffron.

The Valley of Kashmir, nested in the north-western folds of the Himalayas is surrounded on almost all sides by mountain ranges, characterised by snow covered lofty peaks. The mountain range rising to a height of 5550 metres on the north-east dip-down to about 2770 metres in the south, where the Banihal-Pass (Jawahar Tunnel) provides an exit from the Valley. Owing to high elevations there is a continuous ring of snow around the valley upto the end of May and sometimes by the beginning of October. The only outlet for rivers is the Baramulla-Gorge where the placid Jhelum river leaves the smooth grassy banks and hurries headlong down its rocky course to the plains of the south.

The oval shaped valley is filled with thick deposits of alluvium which has blanketed even the lower slopes of the surrounding ranges. It is drained by the Vitatsa (Jhelum) and its tributaries among which the Lidder, Indus, Pohru, Sandran, Bring, Vishav and Sukhnag are prominent. The Valley is about 130 kms. long and 40 kms. wide.

On the basis of stratigraphy and altitude, the Valley of Kashmir may be divided into the following physiographic units.

### (a) The Jhelum Valley Floor

The Jhelum Valley floor includes the flood plains and *Bahil* (loamy) tracts. The Valley floor sprawls from Khanabal (district Anantnag) in the south-east upto Baramulla town in the north-west. The region has rich deposits of alluvium, deposited by the Jhelum and its tributaries. Consequently, it is known as '*The Rice-Bowl of Kashmir*'. The valley is densely populated and it is the hub of economic activities. The agricultural landscape is dominated by paddy and orchards. The valley floor has an elaborate road transport system and enormous potential for tourist development. Almost all the urban places (23 towns) of the Kashmir Division are situated in the Jhelum Valley region.

## (b) The Karewas (Wudars)

The *Karewa* formation is a unique physiographic feature of the Valley of Kashmir. *Karewas* are flat topped or undulating surfaced mounds on the sides of Jhelum flood plain, flanking the surrounding mountain precipices. These are lacustrine deposits and sprawl over an area of about 13 to 26 kms. on the left flank of Jhelum. On the right hand side of the river they are however, not contiguous and have the shape of tableland. *Karewas* are also found in the Handwara and Sogam in the shape of isolated tracts (Fig. 2).

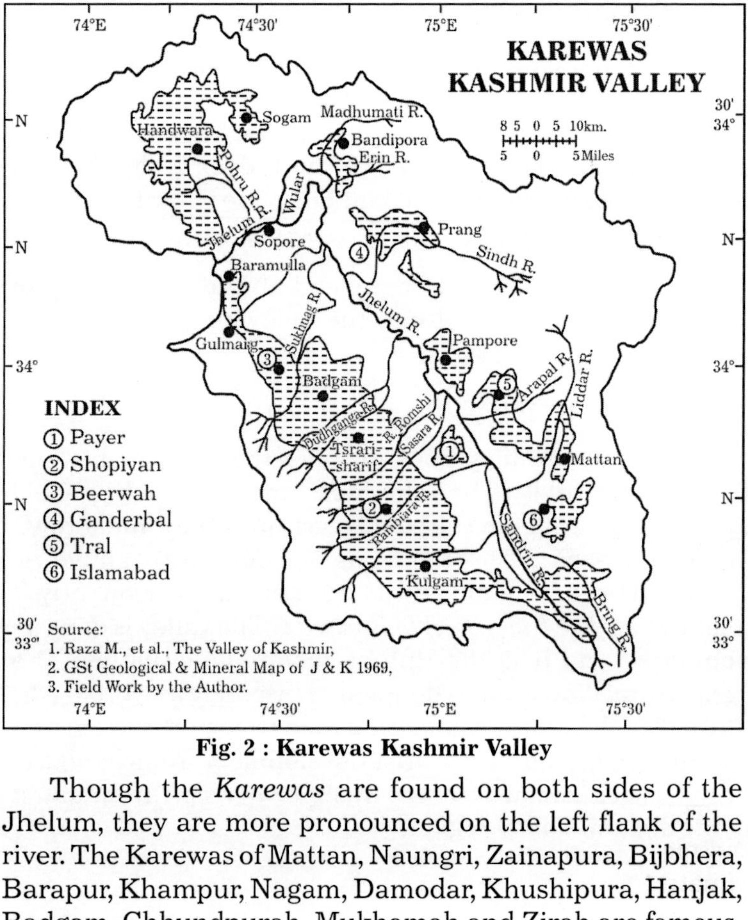


**Fig. 2 : Karewas Kashmir Valley**

Though the *Karewas* are found on both sides of the Jhelum, they are more pronounced on the left flank of the river. The Karewas of Mattan, Naungri, Zainapura, Bijbhera, Barapur, Khampur, Nagam, Damodar, Khushipura, Hanjak, Badgam, Chhundpurah, Mukhamah and Zirah are famous.

These Karewas are situated in Qazigund, Kulgam, Koyul, Pampore, Islamabad, Mattan, Tral, Bijbahera Khushipura, Safapore, Handwara and Bandipore tehsils.

The *Karewas* have deep underground water table and owing to undulating terrain they are not adequately irrigated.

The *Karewas* have great economic and agricultural importance. Commercial cash crops like almond, walnut, apples, peaches, pears and saffron flourish luxuriously in the *Karewas*. The higher reaches are generally under maize cultivation while the flat topped levelled areas aer devoted to saffron, oats, wheat, mustard and rapeseed. Saffron is a perennial cash crop which on an average gives returns for about fifteen years. Interculture of saffron and orchards is an emerging pattern of crop land use in the *Karewas*.

### (c) The Side-Valleys

The Valleys of the major tributaries of Jhelum have been termed as the side-valleys. These have relatively steep gradients owing to which the insolation rate is low and winters are severe. Their soils are immature and deficient in humus contents. Paddy cultivation is confined to the flat irrigated fields, while undulating terraces and *Kandi* tracts are devoted to maize and paddy cultivation. Side-valleys like Sindh, Naranag, Lidder and Daksum are occupied by Gujjars who are largely dependent on pastoral activities.

### (d) The Greater Himalayas

The Greater Himalayas in the state of Jammu and Kashmir lie to the north of Kashmir Division and to north-east of Jammu Division. They separate the valley of Indus from that of the Jhelum river. In the state of Jammu and Kashmir the Greater Himalayas are known as Zanskar. The average altitude of Zanskar Range is about 5940 meters.

The rivers of Zanskar and Sura drain the slopes of Zanskar and merge into the Indus river. The area has most severe climate and as low as – 40°C temperature is recorded at Dras during the winter season. It is believed that Rangdum (Suru Valley) is colder to Daras. Moreover, owing to heavy snowing, Rangdum remains cut-off from rest of the state from November to April. The growing season in the Suru valley is short and the people generally keep goats, sheep and ponies for their sustenance. In summer they grow vegetables, oats and coarse grains.

## Ladakh Region

Ladakh constitutes the northern most administrative unit of the state. It is avast arid table-land located at a height of about 5000 metres. This cold-desert is mostly formed of mechanically weathered rocks and granite dust. It is deprived of vegetation and often been termed as the '*Roof of the World*' where people live at heights ranging between 2800 to 5000 metres above the sea level.

The mighty Indus flows through Ladakh. It is flanked by the Ladakh-Range on the right and the Zanskar-Range on the left. The scanty rains and arid conditions in Ladakh are not conducive for agricultural activities and therefore, cultivation of crops is restricted to the irrigated terraces of Indus-River and its tributories. Settlements are sparsely distributed and their population size is small. Pastoral, and tourism are the main economic activities of the people of Ladakh.

Leh, the divisional headquarters, is situated on the right bank of Indus at an altitude of 3505 metres, on an alluvial fan which has a sprawl of 8 kms. The environs of Leh are highly productive and wherever irrigation has been developed, good crops of grim (a type of wheat) fodder, barley and vegetables are obtained.

In the northern parts of Ladakh lies the Karakoram Range, radiating to south-eastern direction from the *Pamir-Knot*. Some of the loftiest peaks of the Himalayas e.g. $K_2$ or Mt. Godwin Austen (8610m.) are situated in the Karakoram Range. $K_2$ is the second highest peak in the world after Mt.

Everest. Some of the largest valley glaciers are also found in the Karakoram Range. The Siachen-glacier-about 72 kms. in length, and Baltore, Hispar, Rimo, Baifa, Batuna are some of the important valley glaciers of the northern Ladakh.

## Drainage

The state of Jammu and Kashmir is drained by the mighty Indus, Jhelum, Kishanganga and Chenab rivers and their tributaries. Out of the three, the Indus and the Chenab rise well to the north of the Greater Himalayas and they pierce through the main ranges of the Himalayas. The Jhelum has its origin near Verinag in Pir-Panjal Range.

### 1. The Indus (Sindh) River

Rising in the vicinity of Mansarowar-Lake from Sengge-Khambab Glacier, the Indus flows in a north-westerly direction through the trough between the Kailash and the Ladakh Ranges. It is 709 kms. long within India and drains an area of 117,844 $km^2$. It flows for nearly 320km. in a north-westerly directions when it crosses on the south-eastern boundary of Kashmir at an elevation of 4500m. Flowing in the same direction it falls to 3500m. at Leh. About 19km. in the same direction it is joined by the Shyok on the right bank. Near Skardu the Shigar joins it on the right. Giligit river joins on the right further down. Here the river bed is 1220m above the sea level. The river then flows west, crosses the Kashmir border and turns south, southwest into Pakistan.

Indus, though flowing through gorge has numerous alluvial fans and river terraces. The town of Leh is situated on an alluvial fan. To the east of Leh, on either bank of the Indus, is an alluvial plain stretching over a distance of 30 km. This is the most fertile levelled land sprinked with several rural settlement of the Ladakh region.

The flows in Indus are subject to extreme variations. The maximum flow is in summer. The low winter flows are mainly from the ground storage built up during summer. Thus a drought in winter can follow a flood in summer.

## The Jhelum

The Jhelum rises from the Pir-Panjal Range near Verinag. Initially the river flows in a northwesterly direction and after passing through the city of Srinagar merges into the Wular Lake. Emerging from the Wular Lake, it takes a south westerly direction which it pursues upto Baramulla. It finally passes into Pakistan through the Baramulla-Uri Gorge.The Jhelum flood plain is 1585m. above sea leve.

In India it is 400 kms. long and drains 28,490 sq. km. On its right, it is joined by the Bring, Lidder, Harwan, Sindh, Erin, Madhumati and Pohru rivers, while the left bank is joined by Sandran, Vishav, Rambiara, Dudganga and Sukhnag rivers. The maximum and minimum discharges of Jhelum recorded near the Indo-Pak border are as under:

| Site | Maximum discharge | Minimum discharge |
|---|---|---|
| Near Indo-Pak border | 29,600m$^3$ | 112m$^3$ |

## 3. The Kishanganga River

Kishanganga is an important tributary of the Jhelum river. It has its origin in Kishansar Lake and therefore been named as Kishanganga. It drains the Tilail, Burzah–Bal, Gurez and the surrounding regions. It merges into the Jhelum river near Muzaffarabad.

## 4. The Chenab River

The Chenab is the mightiest river of the state. It has its source in the glaciers of Middle Himalayas. At the source, the river is in the two streams, the Chandra and the Bhaga at an elevation of about 4900m. in Himachal-Pradesh. After the confluence, the river flows between the Himalaya and the Pir-Panjal-Range and then takes a turn to the south through a gorge, crossing Pir-Panjal. It flows between rocky mountains till it enters the plains near Akhnoor. The Chenab in the state is 1180 km. long and its basin in India is 26,755 sq. kms. The maximum and minimum discharges of the Chenab river are given below:

| Site | Maximum discharge | Minimum discharge |
|---|---|---|
| Near Indo-Pak border | 15,400m$^3$ | 102m$^3$ |

The rivers of Jammu and Kashmir State constitute a potential source of wealth if properly harnessed and used. A systematic knowledge of the hydrology of these rivers is essential for the purpose. It is perhaps the first step necessary in the planning and development of water resources of the state.

### *References*

1. Wadia, D.N., 1926, '*Geology of India*', London.
2. Raza, M. et.al, 1979, '*The Valley of Kashmir*', Vikas Pub. House, New Delhi.
3. Mittal, R.S., 1968, '*Physiographical and Structural Evolution of the Himalayas in B.C. Law*' (ed.), Mountains and Rivers of India.

# Chapter-II
# Climate

The average weather conditions of sizeable area of the earth's surface over a period of time is known as climate while the conditions of the atmosphere at any place at a specific time or for a short time is known as weather.

The state of Jammu and Kashmir is situated in sub-tropical latitudes but owing to orographic features and snowclab peaks the climate over greater parts of the state resembles to that of the mountainous and continental parts of the temperate latitudes. There are, however, micro-level variations in the general prevailing weather and climatic conditions of the state. A detailed study of climate at the microlevel, in the absence of reliable temperature and precipitation data, is not possible. The general climate of the state can be understood easily by describing the weather conditions of different seasons of the Jammu Division, Kashmir Division and Ladakh Division separately.

## Jammu Division

The southern parts of Jammu Division being for the most part contiguous with the plains of Punjab, has the tropical heat, characterised with monsoon rains and cool winters.

The climate of Jammu Division, barring the high mountains and their leeward slopes is characterised by a rhythm of season which is caused by the reversal of winds in the form of the south-west and the north-east monsoons. The pressure reversal takes place regularly twice in the course of a year. The south-west monsoon in Jammu Division extends from mid-June to mid-October, and corresponds with the rainy season (*Barsat*), while the northeast monsoon extends from mid-October to mid-June. Thus taking into consideration the temperature and rainfall a year in the Plains of Jammu Division and the southern hilly tracts of the Division is divisible into three distinct seasons (*Mausam*):

(i) The cold weather season (November to February),
(ii) The hot weater season (March to Mid-June),
(iii) The season of general rains (Mid-June to Mid-October).

## The Cold Weather Season

During the month of November a high pressure belt extends over the Ganga-Sutlej Plains. Owing to pressure distribution and the influence exerted by the Himalayan relief the prevailing direction of winds in this season is from west to east. The mean minimum temperature in the month of November at Jammu reads about 12°C, but the mean maximum temperature remains about 26°C. The month of December records further decrease in day and night temperature, the minimum occasionally going below freezing point, while the mean maximum reads about 22°C (Fig. 3).

January is the coldest month of the year (Fig. 3). It records the lowest temperature the mean monthly temperature being about 13°C (Fig. 6) and the relative humidity 68 percent. Ocurrence of mist and fog locally known as Dhund and Kohra respectively is common in the morning hours. Intense frost is also observed in the month of January, which affects the crops of mustard, rapeseeds wheat, sugarcane, vegetables and chillies adversely. Irrigation of *Rabi* crops at such occasions is imperative to protect them. February records an increase in the day and night temperatures. This is the beginning of spring in the Jammu region when new leaves appear on deciduous trees like *Shisham*, *Neem* and *Jamun*. During the cold weather season, the western disturbances (temperate cyclones) acccompanied with moderate to intense rainfall pass over the Jammu Division. These depressions (temperate cyclones) have their origin in the Mediterranean Sea. The

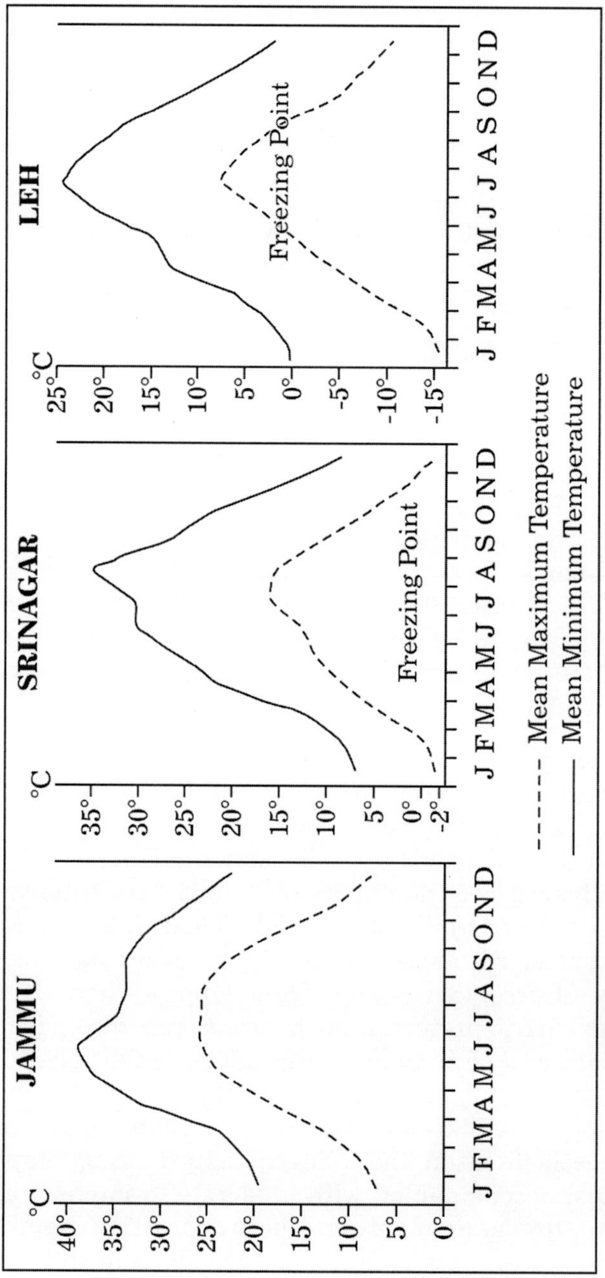


Fig. 3

Fig. 4

Fig. 5

timely occurrence of rainfall in winter season is highly beneficial to the standing *Rabi* (winter) crops. The temperate cyclones are occasionally accompanied with hailstorms which result into considerable damage to the *Rabi* crops of wheat, gram, mustard and vegetables and flowering trees of mangoes, peaches and plums. The total rainfall in the winter season at the Jammu rainfall recording station is about 13cm. (Fig. 7).

## The Hot Weather Season (March to mid-June)

March to mid-June is the period of hot weather season in Jammu Division. March records an abrupt rise in temperature with a continuous fall in pressure. In this month the mean monthly temperature at Jammu is 18°C (Fig. 6). The mean minimum and the mean maximum temperatures read 23°C and 12°C respectively at Jammu, but going up into areas of higher altitudes there is a corresponding decrease in the mean maximum and the mean minimum temperatures. The increase in temperature continues in April and May. The month of May experiences the highest temperature of the year (Fig. 3). The mean maximum and mean minimum temperatures during this month read about 38°C and 23°C

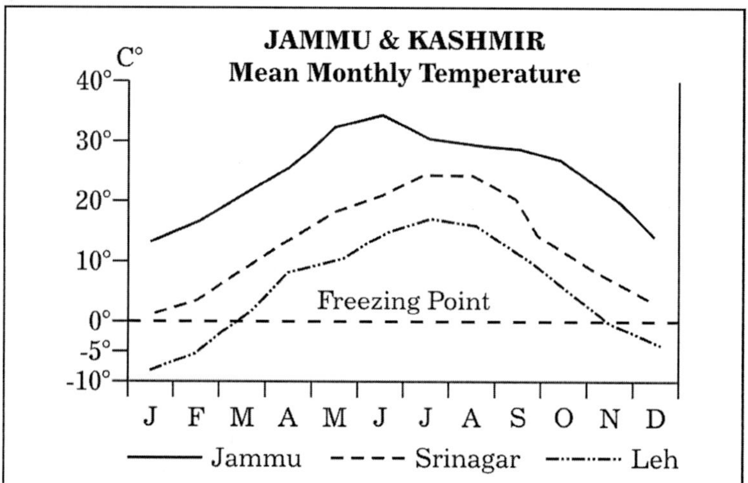


**Fig. 6 : Jammu and Kashmir–Mean Monthly Temperature**

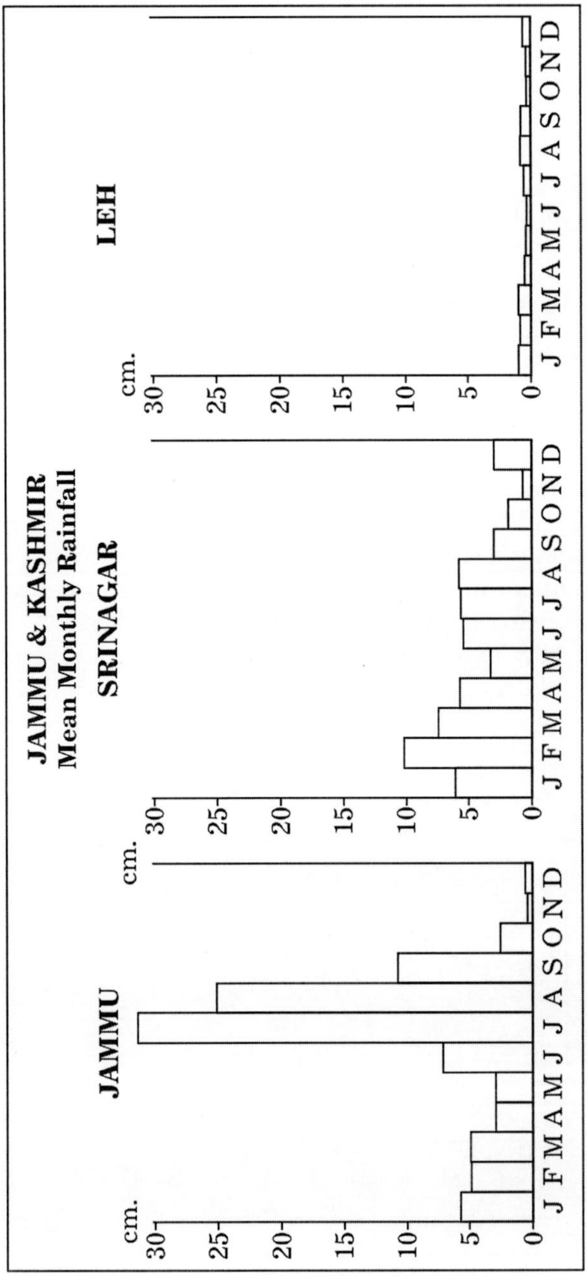


Fig. 7 Fig. 8 Fig. 9

respectively. At Jammu, in the month of May, usually the days are hot and the nights are warm. The relative humidity ranges between 20 to 40 percent, which is the lowest in the year.

In the month of May and early parts of June, in the plain region of Jammu, the surface becomes parched under the impact of intense heat. During this period, hot dry winds locally calles as *Loo* blow which damage the standing crops of sugarcane, vegetables and green fodder. To protect these crops from intense dry heat, they are regularly irrigated, wherever irrigation facilities are available. The ocurrence of duststorms locally known as *Andhi* is a unique feature of this season. The duststorm is characterised by a huge cloud of dust which reduces visibility to a few metres. The duststorms are however, short lived and may result into light drizzles, which modify the weather making it pleasant for one or two days. In Jammu Division, the total average rainfall in the summer season is small (Fig. 6). The rainfall recording station of Jammu records about 11cm. of rainfall during summer season (April-June).

### The Season of General Rains (Mid-June to October)

The season of general rains in the Jammu Division begins in the middle of June, with the outburst of clouds. It lasts till the middle of October. The arrival of summer monsoon rains brings the temperature down and the relative humidity increases sustantially which ranges between 60 to 85 percent. Rainfall alternates with rainless intervals of three to five days in the months of July and August. These are the rainiest months, recording about 64cm. of rain which is over about 67 percent of the total annual rainfall of Jammu (Fig. 7). High humidity and high temperatures make the weather oppressive which may result into the outbreak of seasonal fever and epidemics.

### Kashmir Division

The Valley of Kashmir has continental climate, characterised with marked seasonality. In fact, the genesis of Kashmir weather is intrinsically linked with the mechanism

1. An Overview of Frozen Dal Lake–January 1986

2. Exceptional Showing in Kashmir Valley, February, 2005

3. Shikaras–anchord for tourists

of weather in the Indian sub-continent in general. Nevertheless, the Valley of Kashmir being surrounded by the Himalayan Ranges has a modified sub-tropical climate. In general the Valley has a fairly long period of winter and spring seasons. On the basis of temperature and precipitation a year in the Valley is divisible into the following four seasons:

(i) Winter season (November to February),
(ii) Spring season (March to Mid-May),
(iii) Summer season (Mid-May to Mid-September),
(iv) Autumn season (Mid-September to October).

The Kashmiris, however, recognise the following six seasons with duration of two months each:

(a) *Sonth* (spring) Mid-March to Mid-May
(b) *Grishm* (summer) Mid-May to Mid-July
(c) *Wahrat* (rainy season) Mid-July to September
(d) *Harud* (autumn season) Mid-September to Mid-November
(e) *Wand* (winter season) Mid-November to Mid-January
(f) *Sheshur* (season of severe cold) Mid-January to Mid-March

The Kashmiri nomenclature is based on the empirical experience of the people about temperature and precipitation conditions in different parts of the year, which is scientific and gives a more reliable picture of the weather conditions in the Valley of Kashmir.

**Winter Season (November to February)**

In the Valley of Kashmir, the winter season lasts from November to February. The mean maximum and mean minimum temperature in November read about 14°C and 1.5°C. In December, there is a further decrease in temperature, the mean minimum being 1.40°C and the mean maximum 8°C (Fig. 4). In exceptional years of severe cold, e.g. January 1964 and last week of December, 1985, 1987, 1988 the thermometer read 15°C. Consequently, most of the lakes including the Dal and Wular were frozen and they became the playing grounds for the adventurous sportmen of Srinagar.

January is the coldest month of the year in Kashmir which is locally known as the period of *Chilla-Kalan* (period of snowy cold). Occurrence of heavy snow in the Valley in this month is a common feature. The non-occurrence of snow and precipition, it is believed, leads to various epidemic diseases and scarcity of water in the rivers during the subsequent seasons.

The maximum snow occurs in the month of January. On the average the three months of December, January and February receive about 120cm. of snow, out of which about 50cm. (41.58 percent) is recorded in the month of January. About 6 feet of snowfall was recorded in the valley of Kashmir on 18$^{th}$ and February 2005. This heavy snowing broke the records of last 40 years. The 'White Terror' resulted into large scale avalanches. The avalanches crushed several villages and over 500 people were killed. The worst hit district was Anantnag. The casualty was heavy in Qazi-Gund, Kulgam, Drand, Waltengu, Kapran and Gujjar Basi (Anantnag district). Over 3000 people including army Jawans took shelter in the Banihal Tunnel. Indian Air Force airlifted 20,000 troops over 3000 people and over 100 tourists. The Jammu Srinagar National Highway remained closed for more than a week. People spent eight consecutive day without electricity and water and communication links continued to function with interuptions. Fixed lines and mobile services were hit due to damage to transmission tower. The Dal, Wular and all the lakes were frozen. The Dal lake looked like a playground. Food packets were dropped for about 300 Border Roads organisation and ITBP personnel trapped in the Jawahar Tunnel.

In winters, in the Valley of Kashmir, rainfall occurs from the western disturbances, also known as the temperate cyclones. These disturbances have their origin in the Mediterranean Sea. The rainfall generated by these cyclones is fairly widespread. There are however, variations in the rainfall recorded at the different stations of the Valley. For example, the city of Srinagar records about 30cm of rainfall during winter season (Nov.-Feb.), while rainfall during the corresponding period at Baramulla and Anantnag is 35cm. and 34cm. respectively. Winter rainfall is much higher on either extremity of the Valley, Doru (45cm.) in the north-west receive much higher quantities of rainfall than that of Srinagar. In general, the Valley has highly dreary and monotonous winters with very little sunshine. The relative humidity is generally over 90 percent during this season. To combat cold the people use *Pheran* (a loose woollen garment), *Kangri* (earthen fire-pot) and *Bukharis* (indeginous room-heater). In winters, the consumption of *Balan* (fuelwood) is enormous. The Kashmiris spent a substantial portion of their earnings in the purchase of fuel, wood and coal to be used in winter season. During this period the agricultural activities remain suspended, leading to unemployment. Consequently, many of the laboureres and small farmers outmigrate from the Valley to the relatively warmer parts of the country to seek employment and to pass their winters.

## Spring Season

At the advent of March, the weather starts improving and the temperatures start moving up steadily. The snow starts melting but snowing may take place even in March. In 1983, there had been heavy snowing in the last week of March. March is fairly wet month of the year in which the frequency of western disturbance is high. Srinagar records about 8cm. of rainfall in this month (Fig. 8).

In March the day temperature fluctuates between 10°C to 16°C. Wide variations in temperatures are, however, observed from place to place and year to year. The mean minimum temperature remains around 3°C as a result of which the nights are cool. The weather becomes further inclement at the occurrence of snow and rains.

The day temperature in April and May shoots up abruptly. The night temperature also registers a steady increase. In May, the mean maximum and mean minimum temperatures read about 25°C and 12°C respectively (Fig. 4).

**Table 2.1**

**Jammu–Mean Maximum, Mean Minimum Temperatures and Average Monthly Rainfall**

| | J | F | M | A | M | J | J | A | S | O | N | D | Average/Total |
|---|---|---|---|---|---|---|---|---|---|---|---|---|---|
| Mean Maximum Temp. °C | 19 | 20.2 | 23.4 | 32.2 | 38.1 | 38.0 | 34.2 | 33.5 | 33.6 | 31.9 | 26.4 | 22.2 | 29.39 |
| Mean Minimum Temp. °C | 6.7 | 8.4 | 11.9 | 18.1 | 23.0 | 25.3 | 25.1 | 24.8 | 22.4 | 17.5 | 12.3 | 7.7 | 17.19 |
| Rainfall in cm. | 4.5 | 4.0 | 3.1 | 2.4 | 1.1 | 7.5 | 27.5 | 25.0 | 12.5 | 4.6 | 0.8 | 3.3 | 96.34 |

**Table 2.2**

**Srinagar–Mean Maximum, Mean Minimum Temperatures and Average Monthly Rainfall**

| | J | F | M | A | M | J | J | A | S | O | N | D | Average/Total |
|---|---|---|---|---|---|---|---|---|---|---|---|---|---|
| Mean Maximum Temp. °C | 5.8 | 8.1 | 12.1 | 20.9 | 24.6 | 29.4 | 29.6 | 28.9 | 27.1 | 22.1 | 14.4 | 8.2 | 19.27 |
| Mean Minimum Temp. °C | –1.6 | –0.5 | 3.00 | 8.1 | 11.2 | 15.0 | 18.2 | 17.5 | 10.8 | 5.6 | –1.6 | –1.4 | 7.29 |
| Rainfall in cm. | 10.2 | 18.3 | 20.2 | 5.3 | 8.6 | 3.5 | 11.3 | 3.7 | 1.3 | 1.5 | 0.8 | 1.0 | 84.7 |

**Table 2.3**

**Leh–Mean Maximum, Mean Minimum Temperatures and Average Monthly Rainfall**

| | J | F | M | A | M | J | J | A | S | O | N | D | Average/Total |
|---|---|---|---|---|---|---|---|---|---|---|---|---|---|
| Mean Maximum Temp. °C | 0 | 2.8 | 6.8 | 13.1 | 16.4 | 20.8 | 24.5 | 22.8 | 18.7 | 11.8 | 6.7 | 2.8 | 12.27 |
| Mean Minimum Temp. °C | –1.6 | –13.8 | –8.7 | –4.1 | 0 | 3.1 | 7.2 | 5.6 | 1.2 | –5.1 | –8.1 | –11.2 | –4.24 |
| Rainfall in cm. | 0.39 | 0.32 | 0.28 | 0.23 | 0.22 | 0.18 | 0.48 | 0.60 | 0.28 | 0.1 | 0.04 | 0.03 | 3.15 |

**Souce:** Meteorological Department, New Delhi.

About 30 to 40 percent of the total annual rainfall is recorded during spring season, while rainfall recording stations like Pulwama and Handwara receive about 35 to 45 percent of their mean annual rainfall. Spring rain is often associated with violent thunder-squalls and hailstormes which damage the almond the apple blooming orchards adversely.

In the spring season with the steady increase in temperature, lush green grass develops over the surface and leaves appear on the dormant vegetation. Leaves generally appear on willow and poplar as early as the last week of March and on *Chinar* (maple) in the first week of April. This is the period when the Valley is in full bloom and the almond, apple, peach and pear flowers add more fragrance to the fresh air of the Valley. Agricultural activities which remain suspended during the long winters are again started in April and May. The seeds of vegetables are germinated in the *Radhs* (floating gardens) of the Dal Lake and the *Damb* fields. Ploughing of paddy fields adn sowing of rice nurseries also commence in the early parts of May.

## Summer Season

June to September is the period of summer season in the Valley of Kashmir. The mean monthly temperature of June at Srinagar reads about 22°C (Fig. 6). July is the hottest month in which the absolute temperature on a particular day may shoot upto 37°C. The mean maximum and mean minimum temperatures in this month being about 30°C. and 15°C respectively. Under clear skies and rarified atmosphere this temperature is very oppressive. July and August are the months when electric fans are needed and the well off residents of Srinagar plan their outings for Gulmarg, Pahalgam and other hill stations which record relatively low mean maximum temperatures.

June to September is the period of summer monsoon in the subcontinent of India, but the Valley of Kashmir receives relatively less quantity of rainfall during this season. The Pir-Panjal Ranges obstruct the inflow of monsoon winds in the

Valley. Consequently, less than one-fourth of the total annual rainfall is recorded in this season (Fig. 8).

The high temperatures of June and July help in the rapid sprouting and development of paddy and vegetable crops. These conditions also help in the ripening of *Glass* (cherry), peach, pears and early varieties of apples.

## Autumn Season

September and October are the months of autumn season in the Valley. These months mark a transition from the warm sub-tropical summers to temperate winters. Autumn is characterised by least disturbed weather. In this season the skies generally remain clear, the duration of sunshine is longer and very little precipitation is recorded. It is perhaps the most enjoyable weather in the Kashmir Valley which attracts a large number of tourists from within and outside of the country.

In September, the mean maximum and mean minimum temperatures read about 25°C and 11°C. At the occurrence of cloudes, the temperature however, slumps abruptly. During the last fifty years October recorded snowing five times in Srinagar. In October the diurnal range of temperature is quite pronounced (Fig. 4).

The cool nights and warm days of September and October help in the ripening of walnut, almond, apples and the later part of October is conducive for the emergence of saffron flowers. It is the period when the people collect and purchase *Balan* (fuelwood) for the ensuring winters and harvest numerous varieties of apples. The farmers of the Valley, generally, arrange the wedding of their children in autumn after the harvest of paddy, saffron almond and walnuts.

## Ladakh Division

The climate of Ladakh and Zanskar is very cold, arid and dry. In winters, temperatures are extremely low in Rupsho, the higher plateaus above Tansktse, Rong and Zanskar, while central Ladakh and Nubra possess a comparatively mild climate.

Temperature data available from Leh reveals that the mean maximum and mean minimum temperatures in July read about 25°C and 7°C respectively (Fig. 5). In this season the diurnal range of temperature is significantly high, being about 18°C. Under the rarified atmosphere, the heat in the day is intense and there remains large difference in the sun and shape temperatures. On a particular day the mean maximum temperature may read upto 38°C which may cause sun-burns to the people who work in the fields. In January the mean minimum temperature remains below freezing point reading as low as –1.6°C at Leh and –40°C at Dras. In January of 1986 the mean minimum temperature went down as low as –48°C at Dras. It is interesting to note from Fig. 5 that in nine months (September to May) at Leh the night temperature remains below the freezing point. In Ladakh (Leh) the annual range of temperature is about 25°C. The skies are generally clear and insolation very intense. Winds, however, blow with steady speed and are potential sources for the generation of wind-energy.

The average annual rainfall is only about 20cm. at Leh, most of which is received in the months of January, March and August (Fig. 9). Snowfall is also recorded in the various parts of Ladakh in winters. The snow that falls in winters becomes so powdery that it is swept from the flat roofs of houses with brooms. The ice-crystals, under the extreme low temperature conditions acquire a highly crystalised shape. The dry weather and sever winters are the major constraints in the cultivation of crops and development of agriculture. In the fertile irrigated tracts, however, good crops of cereals, fodder and vegetables are harvested during summer season.

### *References*

1. H. Flohn, 1958, '*Recent Investigations on the Mechanisms of Summer Monsoon of Southern and Eastern Asia*', *Monsoon of the World*. IMD, New Delhi. p. 81.

2. M. Raza, et.al. 1978, '*The Valley of Kashmir*' New Delhi, pp. 61-81.
3. A.N. Raina, 1971, '*Geography of Jammu and Kashmir*', New Delhi.
4. S.N. Bhan, 1956, '*Snowfall at Srinagar*', Ind. Jour. Met. Geophysics VII. pp. 295-300.
5. D.A. Mooley, 1957, '*The Role of Western Disturbances in the Production of Weather over India during Different Seasons*', Ind. Jour. Met.Geophys. VIII, pp. 253-26.
6. R.K. Dutt and M.G. Gupta, 1967, '*Synoptic Study of the Formation and Movements of Western Depression*', Ind. Jour. Met. Geophys., XVIII, pp. 45-50.
7. Monkhouse, F.J. et.al. 1973, '*A Dictionary of the Natural Environment*', London.

Chapter-III

# Natural Vegetation and Soils

Natural vegetation now usually more widely to means all vegetation not deliberately organised or included in farming activity and includes 'wild' or seminatural vegetation. Contrary to this all types of vegetation altered or modified by man directly or indirectly is called cultural vegetation.

The State of Jammu and Kashmir is well endowed in forest resource. Its natural vegetation has great diversity in flora, ranging from the lush-green *Margs* (Alpine pastures) to evergreen conifers on the gentle slopes of high altitudes, and from scrub-jungles of the foot-hills to the deciduous forest on the southern slopes of the Siwaliks and Pir-Panjal Range. The vegetation of the state has undergone a drastic change. Large tracts of forests have been removed through continuous felling of trees to bring more area under plough and pastures.

Forests have numerous productive, protective and bioaesthetic functions. On an average the forests of Jammu and Kashmir yield 6,17,310 cubic million of timber and 1,20,300 cubic million fuelwood annually. Moreover, they fetch about Rs. 65 crores annually to the state revenue. According to the statistics of 1991, the total forest cover of the state was about 18,590 sq. km. The forest area in the different divisions of the state has been given in Table 3.1.

Table 3.1 vividly shows that nearly 60 percent of the total forest area of the state lies in Kashmir Division and the remaining 40 percent in Jammu Division. While Ladakh

Division has only 11.12 sq. km. (0.05%) under forest which may be taken as insignificant.

**Table 3.1**
**Jammu & Kashmir State–Forest Area 20175 sq. kms.**

| S.No. | Division | Area in sq. km. | Percentage |
|---|---|---|---|
| 1. | Jammu | 8123.99 | 40.27 |
| 2. | Kashmir | 12039.89 | 59.68 |
| 3. | Ladakh | 11.12 | 0.05 |
| | Total | 20175.00 | 100.00 |

**Source:** Forest Statistics Division, J & K, 1984.

The sprawl of forests and the species of trees found therein are directly influenced by the lithology, rock-structure, altitude, aspect of slope, insolation and the general edaphic and geo-ecology conditions. The influence of these factors is quite pronounced in the State of Jammu and Kashmir. Consequently, there is great heterogeneity in the flora of the state and marked variation in their density and spatial distribution. The concentration and distribution of forests in the state has been given in Table 3.2.

An examination of Table 3.2 shows that the district of Doda with 26.78 percent of the total forest area of the state is a largely forested district. Baramulla (12.41 percent) Anantnag (11.34%) and Udhampur (11.29%) are the other leading districts which have substantial area under forest. The areal units of fertile plains have large tracts under arable lands and therefore, forest area in such districts (Badgam, Pulwama, Srinagar, Kathua, Poonch) is insignificant. The higher altitudes of the state involve more topographic and geoecological complexities than the plains of the Jammu Division as a result of which forest species and their density differ from slope to slope with in a small distance. In general the southern slopes of Pir-Panjal have thin cover of vegetation while the northern sheltered slopes are covered with thick conifer forests. Ladakh is almost devoid of vegetation excepting the moister strips of rivers which are characterised with stunted trees cedar, willows and fir.

The great heterogeneity in the geo-ecological, pedological and climatic conditions of the state as stated at the outset have resulted into great diversity of fauna. Over 4,000 species belonging to 1500 genera are found in the state. For a systematic study the vegetation of the Jammu and Kashmir State may be classified broadly under the following types:

**Table 3.2**
**J & K State–Area under Forest-Districtwise**

| S.No. | District | Area in sq. kms. | Percentage |
|---|---|---|---|
| 1. | Anantnag | 2289.21 | 11.34 |
| 2. | Badgam | 429.65 | 2.12 |
| 3. | Baramulla | 2504.83 | 12.41 |
| 4. | Kupwara | 1479.68 | 7.33 |
| 5. | Pulwama | 1008.76 | 5.00 |
| 6. | Srinagar | 411.86 | 2.04 |
| 7. | Doda | 5403.27 | 26.78 |
| 8. | Jammu | 1445.49 | 7.16 |
| 9. | Kathua | 789.25 | 3.96 |
| 10. | Poonch | 825.53 | 4.09 |
| 11. | Rajouri | 1296.40 | 6.42 |
| 12. | Udhampur | 2278.69 | 11.29 |
| 13. | Kargil | 11.20 | 0.05 |
| 14. | Leh | | |
| | Total | 20173.74 | 100.00 |

**Source:** Forest Statistics Division J & K (1984).

### (i) Sub-Tropical Forests

The southern parts of the Jammu Division with an elevation below 1500 metres have the sub-tropical vegetation. A great variety of vegetation is found in this zone on account of edaphic factors. These forests have a thick undergrowth of bushes and scrubs. The dominant species of this zone are *Shisham, Neem* (Azadirachta Indica), *Pipal* (Acacia catehe), *Tun, Kikar, Babul* (Acacias Arabica), *Khair* (Acacia catehu) thorny bushes, evergreen shrubs, climbers and tall grasses locally called as *Khar*. Most of these species are broad leaved deciduous type which drop their leaves in the months of

January, February and March before the advent of hot weather season. Apart from fuelwood, these forests are utilized for the roofing of houses, agricultural implements timber. Valuable products like resin, *Katha* and medicinal herbs are also obtained from these forests.

### (ii) Temperate Forests

Going northward as the latitude and altitude increase the place of sub-tropical forest is taken by temperate vegetation. The slopes of Pir-Panjal and Zanskar above 1500m. to 3000m. are dominated by coniferous vegetation, the dominant species being deodar (*Cedrus Deodara*), pine (*Pinus*), silver-fir (*Abies Alba*), spruce (*Picea*), laural, elm and paper-birch (*Burza*).

The northern slopes of Pir-Panjal have the dominance of deodar, blue-pines with deciduous shrubs, while the Jhelum Forest Division (stretching over Gulmarg and Lolab Valley) is dominated by cedar, fir and spruce species of conifers. In the flat valley of Kashmir, *poplar*, *Chinar* (a type of maple). Vir (*willow*) are the main species of vegetation which are deciduous in character.

Most of the species are utilized for fuelwood and timber. The conifers are of great economic importance. These forests produce good quality of timber and paper pulp. The most valuable timber that of *deodar* has been depleted and now confined to the north-west corner of Kashmir Division. The system of farming-out timber to contractors has resulted in the destruction of many fine forests. The tracts which the contractors have spared have suffered at the hands of the Gujjars who with small axe cut down trees partly for the sake of fuelwood, foddar and partly from a kind of natural instinct which impels him to make forest clearings for the sake of grass. Moreover, the inadequacy of hydel and thermal electricity and the sever cold in winters have put the people in position which tempt them to cut trees and their twings. The accelerated rate of felling of trees is leading to the extinction of deodar, spruce, pine and fir. The over exploitation of forests and the use of costly wood for fuel is doing great harm to the state revenue on the one hand and the ecosystems on the other. In fact, many of the ecosystems have lost their resilience characteristics.

**4. Deodar (Oak) the Green-gold**

## (iii) Alpine Pastures (Margs)

The vegetation zone lies between 3600 to 4000m and begins well above the upper limit of conifer forests. Being the zone of high altitudes the climate in alpine pastures is extremely cold over the greater parts of the year. The low temperatures support some dwarf birch and junipers making a shrubby appearance. The stunted trees merge into vast pastures, locally known as *Margs* (alpine-meadows). In these pastures some shrubs form isolated thickets during summer months (June-August). The green and nutritious grasses of alpine pastures are utilized and grazed by the Gujjars and Bakarwals who practice transhumance. These people ascend with their goats and sheep and occupy the pastures in the months of May and June. They stay there upto the middle of September, depending on the prevailing temperature and precipitation conditions. In winters they descend and migrate with their flocks to the zones of lower altitudes of Jammu Division to pass their winters.

### (iv) Xerophytic Vegetation of Ladakh

The high altitude desert land of Ladakh with practically no rainfall over greater parts on the year is largely dominated by xerophytic vegetation. The natural tree elements being largely lacking except for more humid region of Nubra and other side valleys of the Indus river. Hippophae-scrub is the major woody component which is used as fuel and material of roofing of houses.

Taking the state as a whole the specieswise composition of forests has been given in Table 3.3.

**Table 3.3**
**J & K State–Species of Forests-1983-84**

| Forest species | Area in sq. kms. | Percentage |
|---|---|---|
| 1. Coniferous | | |
| (a) Deodar | 1116.30 | 5.34 |
| (b) Chir | 1753.00 | 8.39 |
| (c) Kail | 1795.00 | 8.59 |
| (d) Fir | 3106.76 | 14.87 |
| (e) Others | 11404.32 | 54.59 |
| 2. Non-coniferous | 997.70 | 4.78 |
| 3. *Rakhs* and game reserves | 718.15 | 3.44 |
| Total | 20891.89 | 100.00 |

**Source:** Forest Statistics Division, J & K.

Table 3.3 reveals that nearly 92 percent of the total forest area in under conifers. The most valuable conifer i.e. *deodar*, however, occupies only 5.34 percent of the forest area of the state. Moreover, with the increasing pressure of population the good quality conifers are being depleted at a faster rate. If remedial steps are not taken to check the over exploitation of forests the entire '*green gold*' of the state may vanish by the middle of the 21st century.

In the flat valley of Kashmir, *Chinar*, poplar, (salix sp. and poupulus sp.) and willow are the dominant species of vegetation. During autumn i.e. September, Mid-November, when temperatures are low and soil moisture level increases due to occurrence of dew and frost, these trees drop their leaves. The leaves of *Chinar* are converted into charcoal which is used as fuel in *Kangris* during winters. Many perennial grasses initiate new growth and several annual germinate most of which being suceptible to winter frost lie down with only a few managing to survive in dormant conditions.

From the accounts give above, it is evident that the state of Jammu and Kashmir is relatively poor in vegetation in comparison to other Himalayan areas of the country. The human over-interaction in the form of development of agricultural land and pastures has accentuated the rate of depletion of forests. Whatever, is left of the former vegetal cover, vis-a-vis and kinds of stressess and strains, in the state still has a great importance in regard to soil conservation, besides providing timber, fuelwood, fodder, medicinal herbs and water conservation. The conservation of natural vegetation has to given top priority and it becomes imperative for people and planners to preserve whatever is left. To achieve this objective a sound pragmatic strategy needs to be evolved in consultation with the researches, planners and rural masses. Some of the steps which can help in reducing the rate of depletion of forests may be summed up as under:

The government should implement the forest policy strictly and the wrong doers be brought to the book. In order to reduce the pressure on forests, alternate sources of (hydel power etc.) be adequately developed to provide electricity to the rural and urban population.

Another way of conserving forests is the prevention of waste in lumbering and in preparing the lumber for use. Still at many places much of the waste material is burned which can be used for fuel and some in making small articles like toys and handles for tools. More attention is to be paid to the treatment of lumber with chemicals to prevent its decay and destruction by insects.

Each year forest fires sweep over large areas. This great waste can almost wholly be prevented if adequate attention is paid to safe-guard the forests from fire. In dry season hunters and idle visitors should be forbidden to enter the forest. The burning of forest waste should be done after a heavy rain or snowfall when the danger of conflagration is much less.

In brief a comprehensive forest development plan has to be adopted to increase the productivity of forests, to link up forest development with forest based industries and to develop forests as a support to economy.

## Fauna

As discussed in the preceding chapters, the state of Jammu and Kashmir has great diversity in physiography, climate and vegetation. This diversity in geo-ecological conditions provide the required habitats to varied animal kingdom. The fauna of the state, consequently, differs from latitude to latitude and altitude to altitude. In general leopard, tiger, bear, wolf, foxes, deer, *Hangal*, wild-cats are the major wild beasts. Their population is however, decreasing owing to the over-interaction of man with nature and his encroachment in the forest and natural areas.

*Mushk*-deer (*Kasturi*), monkeys, *Langurs* white-bear, wild pig (*Bad*) have their habitats between 2,000 and 3,500 metres. They shift their place of stay seasonally i.e. in winters they descend at lower heights and in summers ascend to higher reaches, of Pir-Panjals are the abodes of these animals.

Leopard, *Chetah*, wolves and foxes are found in the forests of Pir-Panjal, Lidder, Sindh, Doda, Udhampur, Raisi, Uri, Poonch, Karnah, Kupwara and Naranag catchment. Black-bear is very common in Lolab, Lidder, Doda, Rajouri and Uri tracts. *Barasingha* (Hangal) are also found in these localities.

Snow partiridge, Himalayan-cock, *Chikor* (Kak), cuckoo, larks, *Bulbuls*, quil, storks, parrots, pegion, dove, ducks, *Teel*, vulture, crow, eagle and owls are the main birds of the state. A wide variety of reptiles, snakes, fish and insects are also found in the state.

## Soils

The thin surface layer on the earth comprising of mineral particles formed by break down of rocks, decayed organic material living organism (humus) and moisture is known as soil. It has a physical structure and chemical constituents. Soils may be classified into : (i) zonal, in broad latitudinal zones or belts. (ii) inter-zonal, resulting from special parent rocks (e.g. limestone, sandstone); (iii) a zonal or immature soils, new material on which soil forming processes have not had sufficient time to work.

A soil map of Jammu and Kashmir State, based on scientific data has not been prepared so far. The cultivators recognise their soils by different nomenclatures which differ from slope to slope and in many cases from village to village. The land revenue records have classified soils on the basis of texture, structure and colour. Under the prevailing geo-ecological conditions a wide range of soils both of residual and alluvial origin are found in the state. As stated in the First Chapter, the major part of the state is hilly and mountainous. The outer plains of Jammu and the valley floor of Kashmir are however, covered with alluvial soils deposited by the running water and the fluvio-glacial action. The hilly areas are covered by the residual soils while the upper reaches of Chenab and Jhelum and their tributaries are covered by the alluvial and morainic soils deposited by the running water and valley glaciers. On the basis of rock strata and pedogenic characters the following major categories of soils may be identified in the State.

## Hill Soils

These soils are found in the entire mountainous tract of Jammu and Kashmir Divisions between 700 metres to 3500 metres above the sea level. The steep slopes affects run-off and drainage. Other things being equal, the run-off is large on steep slopes. As a rule more water run-off, lesser its absorption in the soil on steep slopes. The run-off also washes away more of the weathered rocks on steeper slopes. The depth of soil and soil-profile on steeper slopes is consequently, shallower than that on gentle slopes. Many soils in the mountainous areas are shallow, immature and highly susceptable to soil erosion. These soils are acidic in character, deficient in potash, phospheric and lime and therefore need manuring and fertilization for good yields. The humus content vary from slope and altitude to altitude. Depending on the availability of sunshine and rains these soils are devoted to the cultivations of maize, orchards (apple, peach, pears), pulses, fodder and oilseeds. The high grounds are reserved as alpine pastures in which the Gujjar and Bakarwals rear their flock during the summer season. Scarcity of water, leaching, land-slides and avalanches are some of the major problems of the hilly soils which are being accentuated owing to the rapid removal of forest covers.

## Alluvial Soils

In a broad sense, all unconsolidated fragmental material laid down by a stream as a cone or fan, in its bed, on its flood plain, and in lakes, deltas and estuaries, comprising of silt, sand, gravel is known as alluvial soil. In other words sand, silt and mud brought down by rivers in floods and deposited on the temporarily submerged land are known as the alluvial soils. These are the most productive soils of state found in the southern plains of Jammu, the Valley bottom of Kashmir and in the shape of narrow strips and terraces along the tributaries of Chenab and Jhelum rivers. These soils may be classified into : (i) the old alluviums, and (ii) the new alluviums. The old-alluviums lie above the banks of rivers and are generally free from floods, while the new alluviums are frequently inundated as they lie in the flood plains of Jhelum, Chenab and their tributaries. The alluvial soils, wherever, irrigated, grow two to three crops in a year. In the valley of Kashmir these soils are largely devoted to paddy cultivation while in the Jammu plains wheat, grain, rice, mustard, barley, sugarcane, potatoes, barseem (fodder) and fodder are the crops grown in them. Being highly fertile, these soils are giving good crops of High Yielding Varieties of rice and wheat in areas of controlled irrigation.

### Karewa Soils

Karewas are fresh-water (fluviatile and lacustrine) deposits, found as low flat mounds or elevated plateaus in the Valley of Kashmir Bhadarvah and Kishtwar. The important Karewas are found in Kulgam, Shopiyan, Badgam, Qazigund, Tangmarg, Gulmarg, Baramulla, Laithpora, Chandhara, Pampore, Bijbehara, Awantipora, Islamabad, Mattan, Tral and Ganderbal.

Karewa soils are of great economic importance as they are generally devoted to saffron, almond, walnut, apples and peaches, The higher reaches of Karewa soils are under maize cultivation. Wherever adequate irrigation facilities are developed, *Karewas* are also used for paddy cultivation.

In Ladakh the highly weathered rocks under the mechanical impact of insolation and frosting result into fine grained, light coloured soils which are deficient in humus contents. These soils are rich in potassium, nitrate and phosphate and give good agricultural returns in pockets where irrigation water in available. On the river terraces of Indus and its tributaries the soils are of alluvial nature which are being utilized for the cultivation of vegetables, *grim* (a type of barley), small millets, fodder and orchards.

### Gruti

*Gruti* soils contain a large proportion of clay. Its water retaining capacity is high and in the years of scanty rains, it is the safest for rice cultivation. Contrary to this, if rains are heavy, the *Gruti* soil gets compacted and achieves the shape of cakes. Under such scanty rainfall conditions the soil gives poor agricultural returns.

### Behil

*Behil* is a rich loam of great natural fertility. In this soil, the humus content is high, consequently, it does not need heavy manuring. In case of heavy manuring the soil becomes too strong which lead to luxurious growth of plants but poor formation of cereals. On the whole this soil is ideally suited for paddy cultivation.

### Sekil

*Sekil* is a light loam with sandy subsoil. *In Sekil*-fields, if artificial irrigation is available, good crops of rice are harvested. This soil is found on the lower edges of *Karewas* in the Valley of Kashmir.

### Dazanlad

This type of soil is generally found in the lowlying and swampy areas. There are however, isolated villages in which it is also found in higher locations. A peculiar characteristic of Dazanlad is that the irrigation water when stands in the field turns red in colour. If controlled irrigation is provided, High Yielding Varieties of paddy can be grown in Dazanlad successfully.

### Nambal (Peaty soils)

Near the banks of Jhelum river and in the vicinity of the Wular and Anchar lakes is found the rich peaty soil known as *Nambal*. In the years of normal rains and moderate snowfall *Nambal* soil gives good yields of rape-seeds, mustard, maize and fodder.

### Karewa Soils

The *Karewa* soil is generally Gruti. The most productive Karewa land has blackish soil known as *Surhzamin*. The red

*Gruti* is the next best while the yellow buff soil is known as the worst of all. It is found in the *Karewas* of Pampore, Kulgam, Qazigund, Badgam, Tral, Baramulla, Mattan and Ganderbal.

### Tand

Land on the slopes of mountains, reclaimed from the forests is called *Tand* soil. After reclamation under the impact of leaching and soil erosion such lands loose their productivity within six to ten years.

### Zabelzamin

Patches of irrigated land if excessively irrigated lose their fertile character and develop alkaline formations. Such adversely affected lands are known as *Zabelzamin*.

There are numerous other types of soils also recognized by the farmers which include *Kharzamin, Tresh, Limb, Ront, Shath* and *Tats*.

### Soil Conservation

Soils in the State of Jammu and Kashmir, especially in its hilly areas are adversely affected by soil erosion. The removal of organic matter and plant nutrients from the top layer and its leaching by the agents of denudation is called soil erosion. Unchecked erosion gradually leads to poverty of soil and undermines the strength of nations. There are a number of physical and socio-cultural factors responsible for the depletion and erosion of soil. Slopes, precipitation, weather, temperature, wind, snowfall and human action (over grazing, unscientific cropping) all combine to accentuate the rate of soil erosion. To overcome the problem of soil depletion, some of the important devices to be adopted are given below:

The soil erosion can be checked by maintenance of an affective vegetation cover, contour ploughing, rotation of crops, terracing, composting, planting of cover crops, creation of wind breaks (trees, fences), pipe-drainage to prevent gullying, damming of gullies or filling them with brush-wood.

***References***


1. D.H. Davis, 1948, '*The Earth and Man*', New York.
2. G. Morgon, et.al., 1973, '*Human and Economic Geography*', London.
3. L. Symons, 1969, '*Agricultural Geography*', London.
4. Plyurnin, '*Reclamative Soil Science*', New York.
5. M. Husain, 1977, "*Human and Economic Geography*", New Delhi.
6. M. Husain, 1979, '*Agricultural Geography*', New Delhi.
7. P. Kachroo, 1985, '*A Note on Flora of Kashmir, Geography of Jammu and Kashmir*', edt. M. Husain, New Delhi.
8. V. Koul, 1985, '*Changing Vegetation of Kashmir*', *Geography of Jammu and Kashmir*, edt. M. Husain, New Delhi.

## Chapter-IV

# Mineral Resources

The economic prosperity and social well-being of a country largely depends on its mineral, power and human resources. The mineral resources are highly unequally distributed and they are exhaustible. However, large the deposit of a given mineral, continuous mining will exhaust the ores. Men may apply the latest techniques in order to extract every bit of valuable ore, or they may continually prospect new areas to find hitherto unexploited mineral, but they can never increase or replace the minerals that are mined. Minerals are thus finite and exhaustible.

The state of Jammu and Kashmir is well endowed with forest and water resources. It is however, deficient in coal, petroleum, natural gas and basic minerals like iron ore and bauxite. Some of the important minerals found in the state are copper, lead, zinc, bauxite, chromium, gold, arsenic, biospore, kaolinite, magnesite, borax, gypsum, bentonite, limestone, sulpher, ochre, coal, lignite, slate, marble, sapphire, rubellite, quartz and serpentine.

**Coal**

Coal is a combustible rock which had its origin in the accumulation and partial decomposition of vegetation. Coals differ in the kinds, and manners of preservation of plant material (type). They vary in the degree of carbon concentration and in the amount of inorganic impurities. The chief types of coal are anthracite, bituminous, lignite and peat.

The state of Jammu and Kashmir is not well endowed so far as fossil fuel is concerned. Field surveys and prospectings conducted by the Geological Survey of India recently, reveal that lignite, anthracite and peat deposits are found in small quantities. In general, the coal deposits of the state are of the Eocene Age, found in association with nummulitic–limestone (Murree-Series), which have low carbon contents, ranging between 50 to 60 percent.

The major coal deposits of the state are found at Kalakote, Jangalgali, Metka, Ladda, Chinka, Dhansal, Swalkote, Chakar, Dandil, Mohogala and Kura. Coal has also been reported from the Baramulla, Handwara and Pulwama districts of Kashmir. Lignite is found at Shaliganga, Chowkibal and Nichahama.

It has been estimated that Kalakote coal mines have a workable reserve of about 5.4 million tonnes upto a depth of about 300 metres. Analysis of Kalakote coal reveals that it is of low volatile anthracite grade with ash content varying from 10 to 20 percent fixed carbon about 50 to 60 percent. In Ladda and Jangalgali coal fields reserves are estimated to be about five million tonnes. The coal of Ladda also has about 50 percent carbon and 20 percent of impurities and moisture.

The Geological Survey of India has carried out explorations at Mohogala and Metka (Poonch District) and arrived at the result that these places, upto a depth of 300 metres have about 9 million tonnes of coal. The fixed carbon in the coal of these deposit is about 57 percent, volatile 35 percent and ash and moisture 10 and 3 percent respectively.

At present coal is being mined near Kalakote to feed the only Thermal Power Plant of the state i.e. Kalakote. The rated capacity of the plant 7.5MW and 35,000 tonnes of coal is being mined annually in its vicinity. The energy generation capacity of the plant may be enhanced substantially if new generators are installed in the Kalakote Plant and new technology for the mining of coal is adopted.

Lignite deposits are found mainly in the Valley of Kashmir which occur in the *Karewa* formations, right from Nichahom upto Lanlayab. The lingite seams are, however, associated with clays and loams and are interbedded in carboneceous clays in various localities of Kashmir Division. The major lignite deposit are in the vicinity of Nichahom, Chowkibal, Budhasheng, Lanylab, Shaliganga, Raithan, Tangmarg.

According to the Geological Survey of India, Nichahom lignite seams occur from north to south, running over a distance of about 85 kms. The estimated reserve of lignite in this mine is about 85 kms. It covers a width of 16 kms. upto a depth of 8 metres. The estimated reserve of lignite in this mine is about 6 million tonnes. In between Nichahom and Chowkibal a reserve of 8 million tonnes has been estimated.

The total estimated reserve of lignite deposits in the state, according to the Directorate of Geology and Mining is about 85 million tonnes, but owing to thin seams and high ash contents, it is mined only at Nichahom. In fact, the lignite of Kashmir Valley contains only 8 to 25 percent carbon, 30 percent ash, 15 percent moisture and 27 percent volatile matter.

Peat–a superficial accumulation consisting of vegetation matter which has become decomposed to a certain limited extent in the cold regions is also found in the Valley of Kashmir. Its deposits are found in the swampy grounds in the higher valleys. Peat is cut and dried before being used as fuel. It is also applied in field as a manure.

## Natural Gas

Natural gas has not been struck so far in any part of the state. In Jammu Division, areas like Ramnagar, Dharmthal, Nowashahra and Rajouri are under investigation for natural gas. Occurrence of dry gas has been reported by the Oil and Natural Gas Commission (ONGC) in the Kashmir Division. The ONGC has proved the existence of 'dry gas' at the Silk Factory Road, Rambagh (Srinagar). Various indications such as sulphurous water, hot springs, gas seepage etc. have been noticed in several areas of Jammu and Kashmir which prove that in near future oil and natural gas may be found in the state.

## Metallic Minerals

There are a few metallic minerals found in the state. Though at present the state is not producing any significant metallic mineral, there are evidence which prove that gold and copper have been mined in the Ladakh and Kashmir Divisions respectively. The occurrence of metallic minerals in the state is in isolated tracts and in many cases their exploitation uneconomic. A brief description of some of the metallic minerals found in the state is given in the following paras.

### Gold

Gold is one of the rare and precious minerals. It is found in hydrothermal veins in the crust or in alluvial grains, placer deposits and conglomerates.

Gold bearing quartz veins have been found in areas of Dras, Suru and Indus Valley in the Kargil and Leh Districts of Ladakh. The gold found in quartz veins gets exposed under the impact of weathering and may be transported by running water. In fact, particles of gold have been noted as placer deposits in the courses of rivers and streams of Ladakh and the terraces of Indus river. Gold has been traced in conglomerate deposits in the valleys of Dras, Suru and Indus, forming a continuous deposit, ranging in thickness from one metre to four metres. It is estimated that 0.6 gram of gold can be obtained per cubic metre of conglomerate in Ladakh.

### Copper

Copper is extracted from the ore of chalcopyrite which is found in rocks like serpentine, diorite, chloriteschist and slates chalcopyrite a double suphide of copper and iron is the main copper ore found at Sumbhar (Anantnag), Lashtial (Baramulla) and Ganderbal. In Ladakh region native type of copper has been reported from areas of Zanskar. Investigations about the occurrence of copper in Doda District have also been started. It is hoped that copper ore in all the quartz veins of quartzite rocks of the Doda District have appreciable quantities of copper which may be exteracted economically.

## Lead

Lead does not occur in nature as the native metal, yet it has been known to man since the earliest times because of its easy extraction from ore. It is a mineral of great economic importance as it is used largely in various industries.

The main ore of lead is galena. It is found in hydrothermal veins. Galena is a grey coloured mineral. It has shining metallic lustre, relatively soft and very heavy, often crystallising in nearly perfect cubes. Galena and other ores of lead are found in association with slate, phyllites, graphite schist and limestone near Ramsu (Jammu Division). About one million tonnes of galena has been estimated in the Ramsu region.

In the Division of Kashmir, galena deposits have been reported in Buniyar (Baramulla). The ore of Buniyar deposits may yield 30 to 70 percent of lead. Several parts of side valleys of Kashmir are being investigated and there is a strong possibility of lead depostis in the Panjal Trap formations.

## Bauxite

Bauxite is a residual deposit formed under special climatic conditions. It is a mixture of hydrated aluminium oxides, but the name is applied particularly to varieties of the rock laterite rich in hydroxides of aluminium which are the chief ores of the mineral.

Bauxite is a mineral of great economic importance. Being light and resistant, it is used mainly in air-craft industry. In the State of Jammu and Kashmir extensive deposits of bauxite are found in Chhakar (Riasi), near Sangarmarg, Salal, Panhasa, Sukhwal-gali and Khander in the districts of Rajouri and Udhampur. The Geological Survey of India has estimated about 12 million tonnes of bauxite in these fields and the analysis has revealed that the ore contains 60 to 70 percent of aluminium.

### Chromium

The main ore for chromium is the chromite which is found in ultrabasic igneous rocks and serpentinites. The chromite ore occurs usually as brown or black crystal. In the state, chromite deposits are found in Dras, Bumbat, Tashgam and Kargil. It is mainly used in metallurgy.

### Zinc

Zinc is obtained from the zinc sulphide and zinc blende. The mineral is found usually in limestone and veins associated with copper and lead ores. Zinc is found in Buniyar area in association with galena, chalcopyrite and pyrites. Zinc ore is also found in limestones deposit of Udhampur.

### Sapphire

Sapphire is a blue transparent or translucent corundum (gem). It is naturally occurring oxide of aluminium and contains as much as 52 percent of aluminium. In India, Jammu and Kashmir is the only state in which sapphire deposits of good quality are found. The famous sapphire mines of Paddor near Sumjam in Kishtwar are located at an elevation of 4418 metres in the upper reaches of Chenab River in the Doda District. In Kishtwar sapphire was discovered in 1881 and since then mining has been going on intermittently. The precious stone is interbedded in the rocks of Salkhala Series and is associated with meta-basic, intruded by a number of pegmatite and quartz veins. The sapphire bearing portions are lenticulars composed of plagioclase, felspars, tourmaline and corundum. The precious stones occur as small prism of 5 mm width and shows pyramidal structure.

### Ruby

Ruby is red transparent variety of corundum (gem). It is found in the areas of Zanskar, Sumjam and Poddar in association with sapphire bearing rocks. Ruby occurs in metasediments and meta-basic intruded rocks such as quartz and pegmatites.

There are numerous other non-metallic minerals found in the state, most of which are bedded deposits.

### Bentonite

Bentonite is a especial assemblage of clay minerals, in many instances formed by weathering of acid, lavas and pyroclastic rocks. The deposits of bentonite are spread between Bhimber and Kathua in the Jammu Division. These deposits lie, on the gentle dipping slopes of the outer plains of Jammu. Para, Chittopali, Modkali, Uttar Bhimber-Bazar and Panipur are the areas of Jammu Division in which bentonite is found. From Bhimber to Kathua there is a continuous bed of bentonite deposit running for a length of about 10 kms. and about half a metre thick occupying a definite horizon in the Upper Siwaliks.

Bentonite is used for cleaning grease spots, soap making, ceremics plaster, and filling paper, washing silk and cotton clothes. It is also known as 'Serati-Mitti'.

### Kaolinite (Clay Minerals)

Kaolinite is a clay produced by the decomposition in-situ of the felspar. It is the natural (unwashed) China-clay. Kaolinite is found in association with bauxite deposits of Jammu. It occurs between Great-limestone and breccia and Nummulitics and coal measures of bauxite-series of the Salal, Sangarmarg and Chakar areas. The local name of the mineral is *Makol*. It is used for white-washing purposes. Kaolinite deposits are available upto a thickness of one to four metres in the areas of its occurrence which can be used effectively in pottery making.

### Borax

Borax is deposited as a result of evaporation of hot spring water. Ladakh is the only part of the country in which borax is found. In the form surface deposits, borax is found in the Puga Valley and Chumathang of the Maheyang area of Ladakh. Annually about 15 tonnes of borax is obtained from these places.

## Gypsum

Gypsum is an evaporite mineral found in clays and limestones; sometimes associated with sulphur. It is an important non-metallic mineral of great economic importance. It is a hydrous sulphate of calcium. Snow-white gypsum with intercalation of quartzite and schists is found in areas of Uri, Ramban, Assar, Batote. The Uri tract has gypsum deposits of about 30 million tonnes. Gypsum mined near Uri is supplied to the Wuyan Cement Factory of Srinagar (Kashmir). Ramban and Assar fields have gypsum deposits of about 19 and 5 million tonnes respectively.

## Magnesite

Magnesite is a mineral of the carbonate group. It is found in irregular veins in serpentine and formed by replacement of dolomite and limestone. In the State Magnesite is found in Shergol (Leh-Kargil Road). The recent researches by Raha (1975), Chadha (1978) et. al. have discovered good deposits of magnesite in and around Katra (Udhampur) area of the Jammu Division.

## Sulphur

Sulphur is a mineral obtained from iron pyrite or in the neighbourhood of volcanic regions. It is also associated with limestones, sandstones and saltdomes. In the State of Jammu and Kashmir sulphur is found in areas of recent volcanic activity, around hot springs. Substantial deposits of sulphur have been located in the Puga Valley of Ladakh Division. The Geological Survey of India has estimated a reserve of about 6000 tonnes of sulphur in Puga Valley.

## Limestone

Limestone is a carbonate of calcium. It is found in Manasbal, Beru, Achabal, Barwar, Verinag, Wuyan, Jangalgali, Salal, Riasi, Basohli, Kalakote and Khalsi (Ladakh).

## Slates and Phyllite

Slates and Phyllites are the metamorphic rocks of great

economic importance. Slate is obtained from the vicinity of Banihal, Ramban, Ramsu. It is being used successfully for roofing.

In Marpathri near Gulmarg about ten million tonnes of good quality of roofing slate has been estimated by the Geological Survey of India.

### Sand and Bajri

Enormous quantities of sand, pebbles and shingles are available in the Chenab and Tawi rivers and the numerous Nallas and hilly-torrants of the Slate. Sandstones are in abundance along the Jammu Srinagar National Highway and the Jammu Poonch Road in the Siwaliks and Murree tracts which are being used for building materials.

Mineral resources as discussed are exhaustible and therefore should be used judiciously. The exploitation and conservation of mineral resources largely depends on the technological stage, the location of mineral ore with reference to transport and market. The exhaustible mineral resources deserve special attention. A scientific policy about their exploitation and utilization needs to be formulated.

### *References*


1. W.R. Lawrence, 1967, '*The Valley of Kashmir*', Srinagar.
2. D.G.A., Whitten, et.al., 1972, '*A Dictionary of Geology*', London.
3. *Bulletin*, Deptt. of Geology & Mining, J & K.
4. *Digest of Statistics*, J & K, 1984.
5. Chadha, S.K., 1978, '*Sedimentological Studies of the Rock Units of the area between Jangalgali and Salal, J & K State, India*', an unpublished Ph.D. Thesis, Jammu University, Jammu.
6. Raha, P.K., 1975, '*Magnesite in Jammu Limestone, NEWS*'– A.G.S.I. Publication, Vol. 6 (I), Feb. 1975, pp. 5-6.

5. Resort Housing in Sonmarg Kashmir

# PART - II

# SOCIAL PERSONALITY

## Chapter-V

# Major Ethnic Groups

The history of peopling of Jammu and Kashmir State is a record of constant impulses of immigration from the north-west, west, south and east directions. The alien races, ethnic groups and various religions have influenced the cultural ethos and mode of life of people of this region. In the present chapter an attempt has been made to give a brief account of the major ethnic groups of the State.

Ethnic group, in the opinion of Jordon is a group of people possessing a common ancestry and cultural tradition with a long feeling of belonging and cohesiveness, living as a minority in a larger society. Each social group is the keeper of distinctive cultural traditions and the nucleus of various kinds of social interactions. An ethnic group provides not only group identity but also friendship, marriage, patterns, business success, and the political power base.

The mosaic of ethnic group in Jammu and Kashmir State is quite complex and the race structure cannot be explained without understanding the pre-historic movements of people. In the process of peopling of the region, the Dards in the north-west, the Ladakhis in the east, the Gujjars and Rajputs in the south and Paharis in the south-east have closely influenced the existing ethnicity of the people of Jammu and Kashmir. The racial composition of the State was also influenced by the immigrants from the territories of Turkmenia, Tadzkistan, Uzbaikistan, Kazakistan, Georgia, Azerbaijan, Turkey, Iraq, Iran and Afghanistan.

The various ethnic groups of the Jammu and Kashmir State, though intermingled have their areas of high concentration. For example, Kashmiris are mainly concentrated in the Valley bottom of Kashmir; Dards occupy the valley of Gurez; Hanjis are confined to water bodies of Kashmir; Gujjars and Bakarwals are living and oscillating in the Kandi areas; Dogras occupy the outskirts of the Punjab plain, while Chibhalis and Paharis live between Chenab and Jhelum rivers. Moreover, there are numerous small ethnic groups like Bhotas, Gaddis and Sikhs which have significant concentration in isolated pockets of the State.

## Kashmiris

Kashmiris are well spread in various parts of the State but their major concentration lies in the Valley of Kashmir, Kishtwar, Bhadarwah, Doda and Ramban Tehsils of Jammu Division.

'Kashmiri' is a wide term which has loosely been applied for several streams of immigrants, mainly from Turkey, Iran, Central Asia and Afghanistan, and settled in the Valley. There is a close bearing of the Indo-Aryans on the racials composition of Kashmiris. In fact, the Indo-Aryan regions and languages have substantially affected the mode if life of the Kashmiris. The influence of Sanskrit on Kashmiri language is strong and cogent to this day. Moreover, Kashmir has also received racial impulses from Indo-Greeks which have influenced the race structure of the people considerably. The influence of Dards, Ladakhis and Panjabis has also moulded the ethos of Kashmiri culture.

Kashmiris are broad shouldered and usually of medium to tall stature. They are much dolichocephic, have a well developed forehead, a long narrow face, regular features and a prominent straight and finely cut nose. They wear short *pyjamas*, a long loose large sleeved gown locally known as *Pharan*, and a skull cap. In intellect they are superior to their neighbours and efficient in business. In disposition they are talkative cheerful and humerous.

Most of the Kashmiris live in villages and are dependent on agriculture. Paddy, orchards, saffron are the main crops grown by them while the urban Kashmiris are engaged in business, tourism, hotel-management, carpet making, silk industry, shawl-making, wood work, pieper-mashi and several other handicrafts.

## Dards

Dards have a long history. Ptolemy in his book '*Almagast*' has used the word Daradrai for Dards of the western Himalayas. Before embracing Islam, they were the followers of Budhism and Hinduism. At present their major concentration lies in Dardistan (Derdesa), the area to the north of Kashmir Valley, especially in the catchment of Kishanganga north of Sardi, Gurez and Tilel.

In the opinion of Leitner, Dards belong to Aryan stock. This opinion is also endorsed by Ray who states that the Dardic Aryans parted from the main Aryan mass just after their enterence into India. Dardic Aryans then colonised the Pamir region from where they spread to Chitral and Gilgit.

In Physical appearance, the Dards are broad shouldered, moderately stout-built and have well proportionate bodies. In face, they are not handsome, their hairs are usually black but sometime brown, in complexion they are moderately fair. Their eyes are either black or hazel. They are known for their ferocity. In the social hierarchy they are divisible into : (i) Renue (ruling class), (ii) Shins (religious sect), (iii) Yashkun (cultivators) and (iv) Dum (menial class). Dards are dependant on agriculture, pastoralism, cottage industries and trade.

## Ladakhis

Ladakhis have been named as the people of snow-living in an arid plateau, surrounded by mountains, where cultivation of crops is hampered by severs cold and non-availability of water for irrigation. Ladakhis are a mixture of Mongoloid and Aryan races. The Aryans who settled originally in the subcontinent's northern parts were the early Budhist people from Kashmir and the Dards from Gilgit. The Mongolian stock is traced to Tibet, from where the shephereds and nomads came to the valleys of Ladakh to graze their flocks. The present day population of Ladakh is the result of blending together of Dards and the Mongolians.

The recent population data reveals that Ladakh is inhabited by the Budhists, the Muslims, the Hindus and the Christians. The Budhists are mostly the descendants of the Mongolians and bear a close affinity in features with the Tibetans. They are reputed for religious tolerance, honesty and hard work. There are some families even now, members of which follow different religions and yet live in peace. Where the husband wife profess different faiths, the male child is regarded as a member of the community to which the father belongs while the female child is admitted to the religion of her mother.

Budhism does not recognise any caste or racial distinction, but some differentiation is made on the basis of social and occupational considerations. In any case the Budhists may be classified among three principal categories, Namely, *Rigzang, Mangriks and Rignu. Rigzang* is the upper class. *Mangriks* who constitute the middle class consist of *Lama, Unpos, Nangsu, Lorjo* and *Thakshos.* The lowest class which is known as *Pignu* includes *Beda. Mou, Garra, Shinkhan* and *Lamkhun* etc.

Ladakhis are truthful, good natured, cheerful, friendly, industrious and honest. They are seldom angry and soon ready to become friends. In conversation they are very polite. Ladakhis are well built and have developed sufficient resistence to work even when the temperature is as low as –25°C (Chapter 2)

The population of Ladakhis is not increasing steadily, probably owing to the prevalence of polyandry and partly on account of climatic and economic condition which have been operating against the development of population and its increase in number (Chapter 6, Table 6.1, 6.2).

## Dogras

On the outskirt of the Siwaliks facing the plain of Punjab is the habitat of Dogras a distinctive ethnic group of Jammu Division. There is controversy among the social anthropologist about their origin. The major concentration of Dogras however, occurs between the two holy lakes i.e. Saroinsar and Mansar. Lake Saroinsar is at a distance of 38 kms. to the east and Mansar 64 kms. to the west of Jammu city.

In the opinion of some social anthropologists '*Dogra*' is a corruption of the Rajasthani word '*Dungra*' means '*hill*' and when the people of Rajasthan migrated in the hilly tracts under drought conditions, the Rajputs gave this name to the people of hilly country, Sten opines that the name '*Durgara*' is probably a tribal designation like '*Gurjara*'–original of the modern Gujjar, and similarly the word '*Durgara*' has been derived from *Durgara* through Prakrit Dogra.

Whatsoever the controversy about the origin of the word Dogra may be, they belong to the Aryan race and speak the Dogri language. Most of them have Brahmini path and have the sects of *Varnashram*. A substantial section of the Dogras embraced Islam during the 16th and 17th Centuries. At the time of partition of the Sub-continent most of the Muslim Dogras migrated to Pakistan.

In appearance Dogras are short statured, slim and have high shoulders. Their complexion is wheatish, slightly hooked nose, brown eyes and jet-black hairs. The lower castes of Dogras in general have blackish complexion.

## Hanjis

Hanjis the dwellers of water, constitute a significant ethnic group in the Valley of Kashmir. They are mainly confined to the Dal, Wular, Anchar Lakes and the Jhelum river, especially between Khanabal (Anantnag District) and Chattabal (Srinagar District).

There is not unanimity of opinion amongst the scholars

about their arrival in the Valley of Kashmir. They, however, agree in saying that 'Hanjis' belong to one of the ancient racial groups who were essentially *Nishads* (boatmen). Some of the Hanjis claim themselves as the descendants of Prophet Noah. There are historical evidence showing that Raja Pratap Sen introduced boatmen from Sangaldip (Sri Lanka). It is believed that before their conversion to Islam, they were *Kashtriyas*.

Hanjis are sturdy, hard working active people with great imagination. On the basis of occupation and social status Hanjis are divisible into : (i) *Demb*-Hanz (vegetable growers), (ii) *Gari*-Hanz (water-nuts gatherers), (iii) *Gad*-Hanz (fishermen), (iv) *Mata*-Hanz (who deal in wood), (v) *Dunga*-Hanz (owners of passenger boats), (vi) *Haka*-Hanz (collectors of wood from water bodies), (vii) *Bahatchi*-Hanz (who live in Bahatch boats), (viii) *Shikara*-Hanz (who ply Shikara boats), and (ix) *Houseboat*-Hanz The various Hanji groups use boats of different types, shapes and sizes, e.g. *Bahatch, Khoch, Demba-Nav, Kara Nav,* War, Tehakawar, *Parinda* and Houseboat. The type of boat which a Hanji owns and uses for earning his livelihood or the product he deals with to a great extent, denotes his class and social status.

The sex-ratio of Hanjis is about 892 as against 929 the national level and 923 the state average (1991). The low sex ratio shows that the males are better cared and well fed than females. In fact, the females are still a neglected lot an are not properly cared like the underdeveloped patriarchal societies.

A field study conducted in 1984-85 reveals that the literacy rate in Hanji's is only 12 percent. The proportion of literate males and females being 21 and 5 percent respectively. Nearly 34 percent of the total population of Hanjis is engaged in various type of producive activities, while the remaining 66 percent is dependent population, belonging to juvenile, Senile and household female population.

Hanjis is general do not have fixed income. Their income

varies from month to month and season to season. It is more true of those who are engaged in hotel management and houseboat industry. In fact, tourism is an important activity on which many of the Hanjis are dependent. Tourism in itself depends on many other factors like the number and pattern of tourist inflow, the weather conditions and the political situation of the State.

Hanjis, a peculiar ethnic group attached to water in general is not developing at the desired rate. The living conditions of *Gad*-Hanz *Demb*-Hanz are poor and unhygienic, while those who are houseboat owners have better income and social status. Some pragmatic planning is to be made for the socio economic upheaval of the Hanjis of the state.

## Gujjars and Bakarwals

Gujjars and Bakarwals constitute a significant proportion of the population of the State. In general, they have nomadic character and largely depend on flocks and cattle keeping for their livelihood.

The early history of Gujjars and Bakarwals is obscure. There are several theories about their origin. According to one school of thought, before their arrival in the sub-continent they were the inhabitants of Georgia (*Gurjia*) a territory situated between the Black Sea and the Caspian Sea (Fig. 10). Under certain push and pull factors they left their abode and through Central Asia, Iraq, Iran and Afghanistan crossed the Khyber Pass to enter the Sub-continent of India (Fig. 10). In the Sub-continent making a southward march through Bilauchistan they reached Gujarat. Most probably in the 5$^{th}$ and 6$^{th}$ century A.D. at the occurrence of some serious droughts they moved out of Gujarat and crossing Rajasthan and Punjab entered the green pastures of the Siwaliks and the Himalayas. Having their place of origin as Georgia and moving towards the Sub-continent of India they named several settlements after their name, e.g. Gujar (Central Asia) Juzrs (Gurjara), Gujrabad, Gujru, Gujristan, Gujrabas, Gujdar-Kotta, Gujar-Garh, Gujarkhan, Gujranwala in Iran, Afghanistan, Turkmenia, Pakistan and India (Fig. 10). Cunningham (1970) is however, of the opinion that the Gujjars are the descendants of Kusham and Yachi Tribes which are considered to be the tribes of Eastern Tartars Russia.

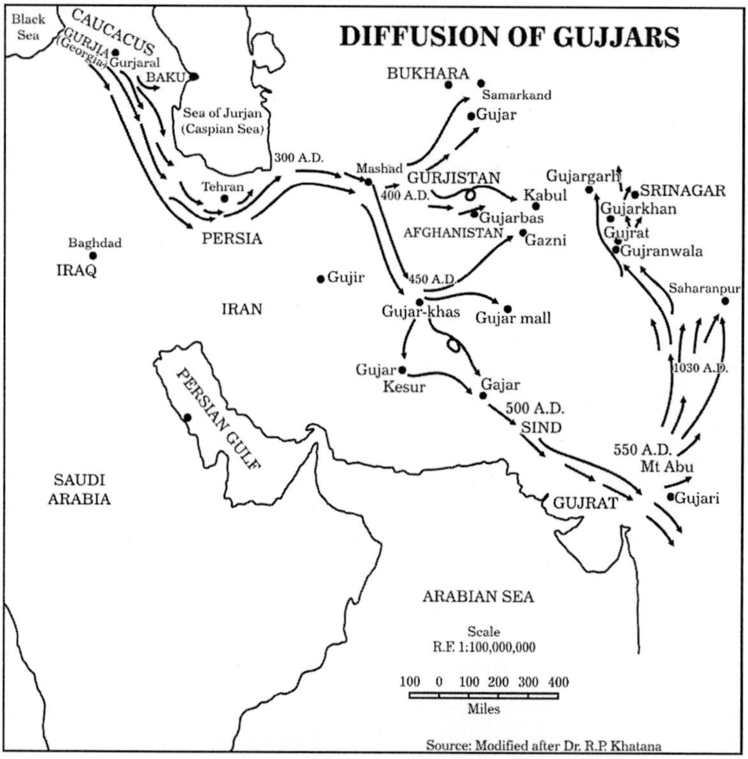


**Fig. 10 Diffusion of Gujjars**

The diffusion and spread of Gujjars in the State of Jammu and Kashmir is not known with certainty. When the Gujjars of Jammu and Kashmir are asked about their place of origin, they simply say that their forefathers had migrated from Gujarat and Rajputana (Rajasthan). The arrival of Gujjars in Jammu and Kashmir is attributed to the outbreak of devastating droughts and famines in Rajasthan, Gujarat and Kathiawad. There are archaeological evidence to prove that there was a spell of dryness in the 6th and 7th centuries in Rajasthan and Gujarat which led to the outmigration of these people (Gujjars), who along with their cattle entered the pastures of the Siwaliks and the Sub-Himalayas. The 'Gujri' language is now recognised to be a form of Rajasthani language, which supports the hypothesis that Gujjars have out-migrated from Rajuputana (Rajasthan).

The major concentration of Gujjars lies in Jammu, Rajouri, Udhampur, Poonch, Uri, Ganderbal, Anantnag, Daksum, Naranag and the *Kandi* areas of the Jammu and Kashmir Divisions. Although some of them have started developing land connections, they are essentially cattle rearers and a section of them–Bakarwals regularly oscillates between the southern slopes of the Siwaliks and the *Margs* (Alpine-pastures) of the Central Himalayas.

In the State of Jammu and Kashmir the Gujjars, on the basis of their occupations and settlements are classified as (i) cultivators who have sedentrized themselves in the sidevalleys, and (ii) the Gujjars who practice transhumance. The second category is further sub-divided into *Doodhi*-Gujjars (milk-man) and Bakarwals Gujjars (who rear sheep and goats).

The houses of the Gujjars and Bakarwals are locally known as *Kothas* and *Bandis*. It is generally a mud-house against the slope of a hillock. The walls are devoid of any ventilation except a small entry door. In one of the walls there is a small hole which is the only outlet for all types of bad gasses and smoke. The shelter though unhygienic protects them and their cattle from severe colds of December, January and February.

The Gujjars and Bakarwals in the State are the followers of Islam, excepting a few who are settled in Bimber, Mirpur and Rajouri. The Gujjars, because of their strict religious adherence, have emerged as the most outstanding tribe who are trusted for their honesty.

So far as the dress is concerned, the males wear a long shirt and a trouser as per the tenets of Islam. Besides, they wear a turban of a peculiar style. The ladies usually wear a long shirt and *Shalwar* with a cap of *Dupatta* on their head.

6. Gujjars and Bakarwals ascending the Alpine pastures (Margs)

7. Transhumance in Jammu & Kashmir

8. Gujjar Labourers at Lunch-Wangat Valley, Kashmir

Though *purdah* system among ladies is not observed, they avoid to face the strangers.

Gujjars are known for their hard work and gentle nature. Rearing of cattle, horses, goats and sheep is their main occupation. They have simple food habits. Maize, milk and milk products are the main ingredients of their diet. They usually start their day with a glass of milk and *Chapatis* (bread) of maize. The same food is being repeated at lunch and dinner. They do not use any type of toxic drinks as taking liquor is prohibited in Islam. Even tea is not consumed by all the Gujjars.

The Gujjars and bakarwals have no written language and no history beyond word-of-mouth tales and traditions. They have no art beyond traditional tribal songs and the simple tribal patterns they weave into their clothes. Although they live on products of their flocks yet some of them cultivate little maize on the slopes in the narrow valleys with spade and hoe. They do not use vehicular transport instead they use draught animals. The assets and resources vital to them are pasture lands, migration routes and water-resources. These resourcs and assets are owned commonly by the tribes and maintained collectively. They have a subsistence type of economy and try to produce everything they need in their daily need.

## Transhumance

As stated at the outset the Gujjars and Bakarwals are essentially cattle, goats and sheep keepers. With the change of season they migrate from the south of the Pir-Panjal to the *Margs* (Alpine pastures) of the Greater Himalayan Ranges in the north. In the seasonal of migration they move with their *Khemas* (tents) and *Rewad* (flocks).

The pastoral economy of Gujjars and Bakarwals is dependent on the availability and utilization of natural pastures. These pastures are markedly seasonal in their occurence. During winter, when the higher Himalayan ranges in the north are covered with snow, the pasturage is available only on the Siwalik-Ranges in the south which has mild winters. As summer approaches the pastures in the Siwaliks dry up, but those higher up (*Margs*) begin to thaw, resulting into the growth of luxurious and nutritious grasses. Consequently, the Gujjars and Bakarwals move back and forth from the lower Himalayas to the pastures in the Upper-Himalayan region. In their movements, they follow well defined tracks known as Rasto from *Sardiyon ki Charagah* (winter pastures) to the *Dhoks* (summer pastures). In this process they drive large *Rewads* (flock) through snow clad *Galis* (mountain-passes), over the ridges, steep slopes, spurs, streams and rivers. They have developed an annual set schedule of activities, and seasonal migration along with *Paraos* (halts), departures, duration of occupation of different *Paraos* round the year.

The Gujjars and Bakarwals follow either the Pir-Panjal Pass or the Banihal Pass Route in their seasonal migration. A brief description of these routes and the problems confronted by them on their way have been given in the following paras.

## The Pir-Panjal Route

The *Qafilas* of Gujjars who follow the Pir-Panjal Pass Route start in the third week of April and take about sixty days to reach the destination-*Dhoks* (Alpine pastures). Out of the sixty days 22 are journey days and 38 halt days. The Qafilas start from Lamberi and making halts at suitable pastures pass through Sialsui, Kesargala, Dangri, Rajouri, Sao, Thana-Mandi and Neelderi (Fig. 11-A), At Neelderi they stay for about two weeks and this period of stay is utilized for grazing salt etc. is given to sheep, the equipments are repaired and they purchase articles or household.

From Neelderi they move to Mara, Chandimar, Poshiana and cross the stream of Chitta-Pani in which ice pieces flow with water. In this track they face a lot of difficulties in fording the Chitta-Pani stream. Moreover, in this tract at the occurrence of rains and hails, the flocks face great hardship.

From Poshiana they move to Gadar-Maidan, and it is in this tract where the Pir-Panjal Pass is crossed. Subsequently, they move from Gadar-Maidan to Sangerveni and then Shalimar to the north-east of Srinagar. From Shalimar they proceed towards Wayil, Wangat and Narang catchment. From Naranag the flocks ascend towards Gadsar. Gadsar is the summer base of this group and they graze their goats and sheep in whole summer in the pastures situated in the vicinity of Gadsar (Fig. 11-A).

## The Banihal Route

The Gujjars and Bakarwals who follow the Banihal Route also cover the distance from Siwaliks to Alpine pastures in about sixty days. On the way they break their journeys at twelve places (Fig. 11-B).

These *Qafilas* start their upward journey in the middle of April, preferably on Friday or Monday. They start from Kirangyal and break the journeys at Manawal, Katta (Ladhadhar intervening pasture), Surinkund, Kabikhattar, Khattar. Banihal, Dingunar, Achhabal, Salar, Mastnar, Girwar, Chandanwari, Gabdalwa, Panjtarni, Kibalnari and Sokhnalla (Fig. 11-B).

The journey between Khattar to Banihal is full of anxiety and tension as the flocks are to be taken on the Jammu-Srinagar National Highway. This is a continuous 23 hours Journey. The herdsmen remain under tension on this track because of the fear of accidents, animal lifters and lack of fodder. This journey is broken at the Shaitani-Nalla (Banihal) for one day for rest after a long and hazardous journey. Crossing the Banihal Tunnel, the *Qafilas* enter the Valley of Kashmir and through Verinag, Aishmuqam, reach Daksum, Chandanwari, Sukhnala pastures (Fig. 11-B).

The return journey for the winter pastures (Siwaliks of Jammu) commences in autumn in the month of September. It is the period when night temperature in the Alpine-pastures reaches fairly close to the freezing point and occurrence of frost is a common phenomenon. The green

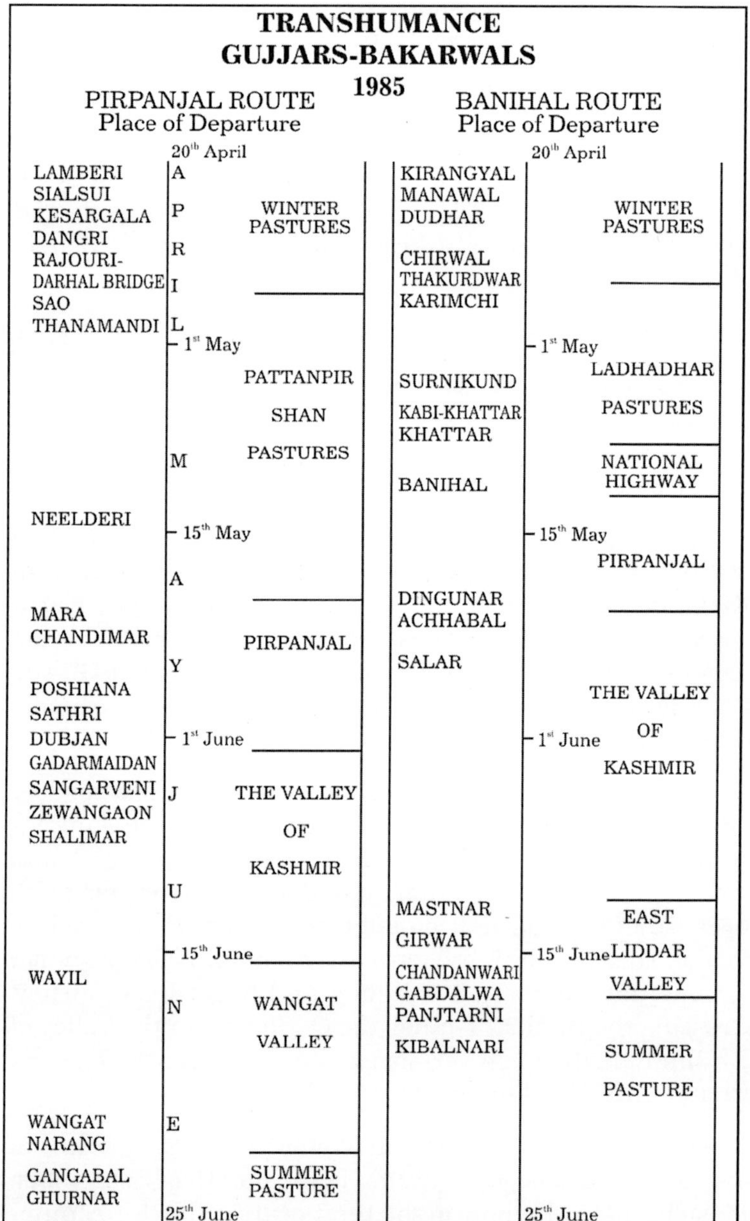


**Source:** 1. Modified after R.P. Khatana
2. Field work by the author

**Fig. 11-A** **Fig. 11-B**

pastures die under the impact of frost. Protection from cold is essential for the herds and the herdsmen and therefore they start descending for the winter pastures. The return journey also takes almost two months which is broken at the traditional *Paraos* (halts).

This oscillation of herds and herdsmen is a peculiar phenomenon of the Gujjars and Bakarwals in the State of Jammu and Kashmir. It has its own merits and demerits. The flock and Bakarwals face a lot of difficulties while making risky and hazardous journeys through the snow covered passes and the busy National Highway. Nevertheless, this is a way of life which cannot be stopped completely. In fact, it is a away of life and there are cogent reasons behind the practice of transhumance. The climate, the terrain, their food habits, their needs, self-reliance and their land connections have a say on transhumance. The whole gamut of primitive society is interwoven with the flocks and their products. In other words their way of life, training of youth, social and political systems, the ceremonies and festivals, and in brief their philosophy of life are the products of cattle and flock rearing economy. This is when many of the new projects and plans initiated for the welfare could not bring the desired results. They cannot be sedentrized easily and therefore any scheme to bring change in their society should be gradual and smooth, causing least disturbance in their traditional mode of life.

### *References*

1. H.N. Koul, 1958, '*A Survey of the Origin of People of Kashmir*', Kashmir Today, Vol. II. 9, p. 18.
2. P.N.K. Bamzai, 1962, '*History of Kashmir*', Delhi, p. 4.
3. V. Kumari, 1968, '*The Nilmat Purana*', Vol. I. Jammu, pp. 22-23.
4. C.E. Bates, '*A Gazetteer of Kashmir*', Jammu, p. 1.
5. M.A. Stein, 1979, '*Kalhan's Rajtarangani*', p. 386.
6. G.M.D. Sufi, 1979, '*Islamic Culture in Kashmir*', New Delhi, pp. 3-9.

7. S.C. Ray, 1970, '*Early History and Culture of Kashmir*', pp. 26-34.
8. F. Drew, 1971, '*The Territories of Jammu & Kashmir*', Delhi.
9. L.Rookh Rub, '*Race and Tribes–Culture of Kashmir*', New Delhi.
10. W.R. Lawrance, 1967, '*The Valley of Kashmir*', Srinagar.
11. *Imperial Gazetteer of India*, Vol. XV, 1908, London.
12. J. Pathik, 1980, '*Cultural Heritage of Dogras*', New Delhi.
13. S.S. Shashi, '*The Nomads of Himalayas*', Delhi, p. 20.
14. M.K. Koul, '*Gujjars the Lords of Jungles*', Kashmir Today, Vol. IV, 9, pp. 7-8.
15. R.P. Khatana, 1985, '*Gujara-Bakarwal Transhumance in Jammu and Kashmir Himalayas : Responses of Spring Migrations*', in Geography of Jammu & Kashmir, ed. M. Husain, New Delhi, pp. 86-115.
16. M. Husain, 1985, '*Major Ethnic Groups of Jammu & Kashmir*', Geography of Jammu & Kashmir.
17. M.L. Lidhoo, 1985, '*Gujjars-Their Attitude Towards Social Changes, Education and Modernization*', pp. 2-21.
18. A. Mam ,1974, '*Hanjis of Dal Lake*', unpublished, M. Phil. Dissertation, University of Kashmir.

## Chapter-VI

# Population

As discussed in the foregoing chapters, the state of Jammu and Kashmir has great diversity in its terrain, climatic conditions and resource base. These variations have resulted into uneven distribution of population. In fact, nearly 85 percent of the total population of the state is concentrated in the Jammu Plains, Jhelum-Valley and along the National Highways, while the remaining 15 percent is sprinkled in the side valleys and Kandi lands. Contrary to this the Greater Himalayas, Zanskar and Ladakh ranges are the negative areas which have insignificant distribution of population. Thus the spatial distribution of population shows a rigid environmental control.

The population of Jammu and Kashmir was 10,069,917 constituting only 0.99 percent of the total population of India. Out of this 53,00,574 were males and 47,69,343 females. The density of population 2001 was 100 persons per sq. km. as against 77 per sq. km. in 1991. The growth rate of population between 1991-2001 was about 29.04 percent and the sex ratio in the state was 900/1000. According to the census of 2001 the overall literacy rate was 55.52 percent. The male and female literacy being 66.60 and 43.00 percent respectively. The increase in population is a direct outcome of births and deaths as imigration of people is very limited in the state. The agricultural density of population also reveals a close relationship with the fertility and the carrying capacity of land. Obviously, the density, like distribution is a function of many physico-socio-economic and political factors.

## Population Growth

In India the population census is being carried on since 1871, but reliable date on the population of Jammu and Kashmir is available only after 1951. In general prior to 1921, the population of the state grew at a slow rate. This was because the state experienced a number of famines and epidemics. After 1921, however, the population increased steadily. In 1951, just after the partition, the population of the state was 32.5 million. In 1961 it grew to 35.6 million, while in 1971 increased to 46.1 million. According to the last census 2001 the total population of the state was 10,143,700 constituting only 0.99 percent to the total population of India.

The phenomenal increase in the population of the state is because of a rapid fall in death rate. The development and extension of medical facilities have not only reduced the death rate, it has also increased the life span of the people.

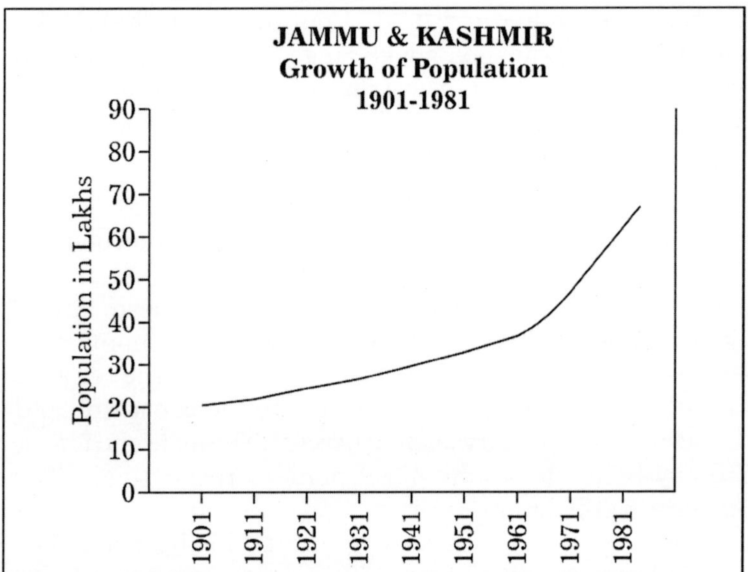


**Fig. 12 : Jammu and Kashmir–Growth of Population 1901-1981**

An analysis of Table 6.1 shows that the estimated population in 1951 was about 3.25 million. In 1951, owing to certain special political conditions no enumeration of population was done. Between 1951 and 1961 the population grew by about nine and a half percent. The increase in population had been phenominal between 1961-71 and 1971-81, showing a growth rate of over 29 percent (Table 6.1). This stupendous growth of population may put enormous burden on the resource base of the state which may ultimately lead to serious population problems and ecological imbalances.

**Table 6.1**
**Jammu & Kashmir State–Growth of Population**

| Year | Population in million | Growth Rate |
|---|---|---|
| 1951 | 32.5* | — |
| 1961 | 35.6 | 9.54 |
| 1971 | 46.1 | 29.49 |
| 1981 | 59.5 | 29.06 |
| 1991* | 77.19* | 29.95* |
| 2001 | 100.69 | 29.04 |

*Estimated Population

**Source:** Census of India, 1951-2001.

As discussed in the foregoing paras the distribution pattern of population has generally been controlled closely by the terrain, topography, availability of water, climate and fertility of soils. The district-wise distribution of population of the state has been given in Table 6.2.

**Table 6.2**
**Population Distribution—District-wise–2001**

| District | Population | Percentage | Total |
|---|---|---|---|
| 1. Doda | 6,90,474 | 7.00 | |
| 2. Jammu | 15,71,911 | 16.00 | |
| 3. Kathua | 5,44,206 | 5.00 | |
| 4. Poonch | 3,71,561 | 4.00 | |
| 5. Rajouri | 4,78,595 | 5.00 | |
| 6. Udhampur | 7,38,965 | 7.00 | |
| Jammu Division | 43,95,712 | — | 44.00 |
| 7. Anantnag | 11,70,013 | 12.00 | |
| 8. Badgam | 5,93,768 | 6.00 | |

| | | | |
|---|---|---|---|
| 9. Baramulla | 11,66,722 | 12.00 | |
| 10. Kupwara | 6,40,013 | 6.00 | |
| 11. Pulwama | 6,32,295 | 6.00 | |
| 12. Srinagar | 12,38,530 | 12.00 | |
| Kashmir Division | 54,41,341 | — | 54.00 |
| 13. Leh | 1,17,637 | 1.00 | |
| 14. Kargil | 1,15,227 | 1.00 | |
| Ladakh Division | 2,32,864 | — | 2.00 |
| Total J & K State | 10,069,917 | 100.00 | 100.00 |

**Source:** Census of India, 2001.

An examination of Table 6.2 reveals that 54 percent of the total population of the state is concentrated in the Kashmir Division and 44 percent in Jammu Division, while only 2 percent resides in the Division of Ladakh. Jammu and Srinagar Districts with 16 percent and 12 percent of the total population respectively have heavy concentration of population. In fact, Srinagar and Jammu cities are growing at a phenomenal pace. These cities being the centres of administration and socio-cultural and economic activities, have better social amenities which attract people from the neighbouring towns and villages. Contrary to this the districts of Leh, Kargil and Doda have little attraction for the people as a result these areas are very sparsely populated.

The average density of population per sq. km. given in Table 6.3 gives a picture of the density of population and that of households. The average density of population of Jammu and Kashmir was 100 persons per sq. km. in 2001 as against the national average of 324 persons per sq. km. In other words the state is fairly sparsely populated as compared to the country as a whole. Within the state there are, however, glaring disparities in the density of population. There are four districts namely Srinagar, Jammu, Pulwama and Badgam in which the average density of population is much higher to that of the national level (Table 6.3). In Anantnag Baramulla, Kathua, Kupwara, Poonch, Rajouri, Doda and Udhampur also the density of population is over 100 persons per sq. km. There are two districts (Kargil, Leh) in which the density is much below the state level. Kargil and Leh with a density of 8 and 3 persons per sq. km. respectively are the least populated districts of the state. The difficult terrain, very cold winters, harsh climatic conditions, aridity and poor accessibility are the main factors for this sparse distribution of population in these districts.

**Table 6.3**
**Jammu and Kashmir—Density of Population 2001**

| Uni | Density of Population per sq. km. | No. of Households per sq. km. |
|---|---|---|
| All India | 324 | 38.79 |
| J & K | 100 | 9.27 |
| Srinagar | 556 | 46.33 |
| Jammu | 508 | 52.63 |
| Pulwama | 452 | 41.76 |
| Badgam | 433 | 39.75 |
| Anantnag | 294 | 24.57 |
| Baramulla | 254 | 21.03 |
| Kathua | 205 | 23.19 |
| Kupwara | 269 | 21.47 |
| Poonch | 222 | 20.65 |
| Rajouri | 182 | 18.48 |
| Udhampur | 162 | 17.47 |
| Doda | 59 | 5.71 |
| Kargil | 8 | 0.88 |
| Leh | 3 | 0.33 |

**Source:** Census of India, 2001
Digest of Statistics, Directorate of Economics and Statistics. J& K.

The number of household given in the third column of Table 6.3 also reveals an identical pattern. Srinagar, Jammu, Pulwama and Badgam districts have about 40 or more households per sq. km. The state average of households per sq. km. was 9.27 Doda, Kargil and Leh have less than 9.27 households per sq. km. and thus further supports the point of geo-ecological control on the density of households in the various administrative units of the State.

## Population Characteristics

Apart from birth rate, death rate and growth rate, the size, age and sex composition, literacy rate, religious composition, longerity occupational structure and migration are the major attributes of population which determine the economic development and social well-being of the respective population. In the following paras, a brief account of some of these characteristics of population of the state have been given.

## Age Structure

Age composition has a direct bearing on the occupational structure and dependency ratio of a population group. The age structure of the Jammu and Kashmir State has been plotted in the shape of pyramid in Fig. 13.

The age and sex pyramid of the state (Fig. 13) is typical of the underdeveloped societies i.e. a very broad base and a tapering top. Nearly 42 percent of the state's population is below the age of 15 years and only 8 percent above the age of 59. In other words, 50 percent of the population is in active age group thus each worker is supporting 1 persons besides himself.

## Sex Composition

The role of an individual in a family or society is deeply associated with the age and sex. The sex-ratio of a social group is largely determined by a large number of bio-social and cultural factors which include the differential death rates among the two sex and the sex selective migration.

The state has a sex ratio of 900 females per thousand of males as against the national average of 933 (2001). Apart from biological factors, the low sex-ratio is due to high mortality in females. The spatial distribution of sex ratio reveals a high degree of variation. For example, the Division of Kashmir has only 879 females per thousand of males, while in Jammu Division this ratio is 925. In Ladakh the sex ratio is at par to the state average. The Division of Kashmir in

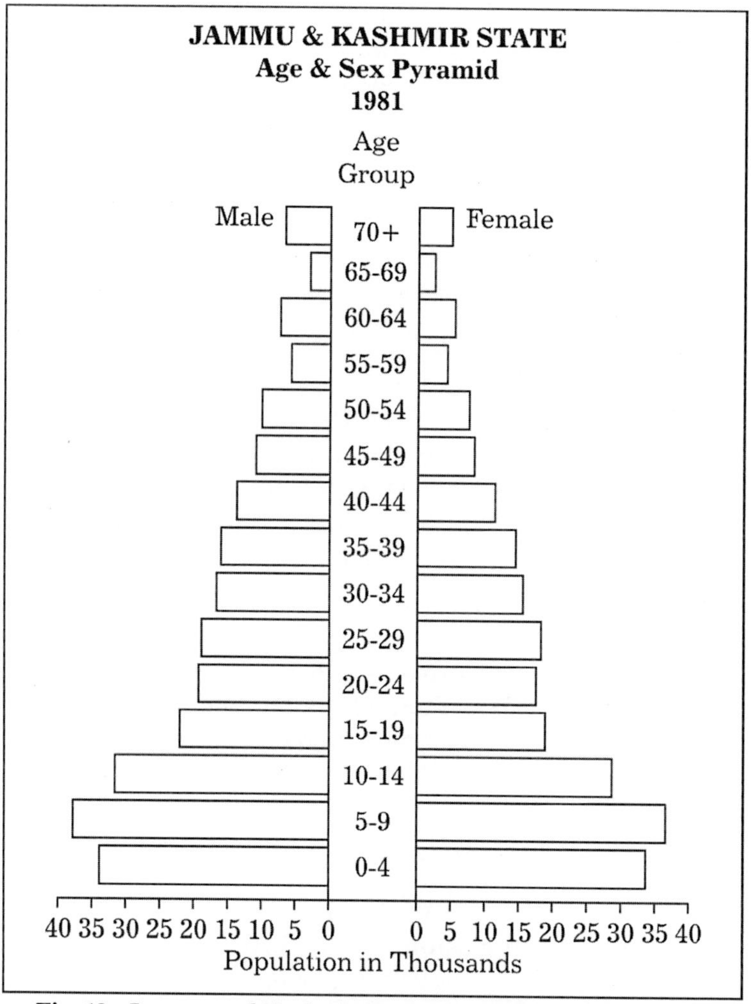


**Fig. 13 : Jammu and Kashmir State–Age & Sex Pyramid 1981**

which 94 percent of the total population is Muslim by faith has low literacy rate. Consequently, the female babies are not properly cared which leads to high mortality rate. Contrary to this in Jammu Division Hindu population has high concentration in which high literacy and education lead to more care of females, affecting favourably the sex-ratio. The sex ratio in Jammu Division in the age group of 0 to 6 years age group is declining fast which shows a discrimination against the female babies. It has been found that sex-determination before birth has become a popular practice among the rich people of the Jammu Division.

## Literacy Rate

Literacy has been defined in the census of India as the ability to read and write with understanding. In the census of 2001, a person aged seven and above, who can both read and write with understanding in any language, is considered as literate. In census prior to 1991, children below five years of age were necessarily treated as illiterate. Literacy reflects the socio-economic and cultural set up of a class or community. Literacy rate affects the fertility, mortality rates, marriages and the level of participation in the economic activities. Literacy accelerates the process of economic change, employment and job opportunities, and occupational mobility from primary to secondary and tertiary sectors. The literacy rate of Jammu and Kashmir state at the district level has been shown in Table 6.4.

An examination of Table 6.4 shows that according to the Census of 2001, 55.52 percent of the total population of the state was literate as against 64.84 percent for the country as a whole. The percentage of male and female literacy rate was 66.60 and 43.00 percent respectively.

The literacy rate of the state has been given in Table 6.4

**Table 6.4**
**Jammu and Kashmir State–Literacy Rate, Districtwise, 2001**

| India | Literacy Rate Percentage |
|---|---|
| All India | 64.84 |
| J & K | 54.46 |
| Jammu | 77.3 |
| Kathua | 65.29 |
| Leh | 62.24 |
| Srinagar | 59.31 |
| Rajouri | 57.65 |

| | |
|---|---|
| Udhampur | 54.16 |
| Poonch | 51.07 |
| Pulwama | 47.35 |
| Doda | 46.92 |
| Baramulla | 44.57 |
| Anantnag | 44.10 |
| Kupwara | 40.80 |
| Badgam | 39.57 |

**Source:** Census of India, 2001

The highest literacy rate was recorded in the district of Jammu (77.3%) followed by Kathua 65.29% and Leh 62.24%. Srinagar district with 59.31% literacy rate was much below the literacy rate of the national average 64.84%. The lowest literacy was found in Badgam (39.54%), while in the rest of the districts it ranged between 40 and 59% (Table 6.4). The literacy rate in the state has improved steadily.

In the state of Jammu and Kashmir, unfortunately, there is an increase in the number of illiterates with the passage of time. The economic development and human progress of a society is not possible without education. It is, therefore, imperative to provide this facility to the entire population of the state and efforts be made to educate the younger generation of the people like Gujjars and Bakarwals who practice transhumance. The socially backward and economically deprived people deserve especial attention for removing illiteracy from the tradition bound social groups of the state.

## Religious Composition

Religious is an important cultural features of a population. Throughout the history of mankind, it has furnished as a motivating force. It is concerned mainly with the wellbeing of mankind on earth. All religious have left an imprint on the customs, art, literature, food-habits, politics and culture of mankind. It has been a divisive as well as unifying force. The religious composition of the state has been analysed in the following paras.

The percentage distribution of the population by various religious shows that Muslims constitute about 65% of the total population of the state. Hindus rank second with 30.41%. There are 1.26% Buddhist, 1.06% Sikhs and 0.19% Christians, Jains and others.

The religious composition of the Jammu and Kashmir State has been given in Table 6.5.

**Table 6.5**
**Jammu and Kashmir State–Religious Composition-1991**

| Division | Muslims % | Hindus % | Sikhs % | Budhists % | Others |
|---|---|---|---|---|---|
| Kashmir | 94.00 | 4.42 | 1.20 | 0.05 | 0.33 |
| Jammu | 33.81 | 62.06 | 3.67 | 0.11 | 0.35 |
| Ladakh | 44.66 | 0.01 | — | 1.82 | 3.51 |
| Total | 65.84 | 30.41 | 1.06 | 1.26 | 0.19 |

**Source:** Census of India, 1991.

Though Muslims have an overall majority but the Jammu Division has a very high concentration of Hindus and in Ladakh the Buddhists ara the dominant religious group.

In the Kashmir Division about 94% of the total population is Muslim by faith. Hindus and Sikhs come next with 4.42% and 1.2% of the total population respectively. There are spatial variations in the distribution of Muslims in the Valley of Kashmir. For example, there are five Tehsils (Sonawari, Chadura, Karnah, Ganderbal and Bandipora) in which over 98% of the total population is Muslim. In the remaining tehsils also the percentage of Muslims varies between 90 to 98 excepting Srinagar Tehsil in which this percentage is 87.

The Division of Jammu, especially the southern plains are dominated by Hindus in which, they constitute over 62% of the total population. Going northward in the Division the population of Muslims becomes significant. In fact, the Tehsil of Kishtwar, Bhadarwah, Doda, Banihal, Ramban, Riasi, Gul-Gulabgarh, Naoshahra, Rajouri and Poonch have a significant concentration of Muslim Population.

Ladakh is very sparsely populated. The Ladakh Division has about 52% Buddhists and nearly 45% Muslims. In this Division Hindus and others are almost absent. The district of Leh has a high concentration of Buddhists while Kargil District is dominated by Muslims.

## Occupational Structure

Occupational structure means the division of working population in different occupations and professions. The quality of work and the regularity of employment in the primary, secondary and tertiary sectors reflect the economic development of a region. The total population of an area is sub-divided into : (i) the economically active, and (ii) inactive population. The economically active group is called as labour force or working population. Larger the size of workers, greater is the generating demand and an increase in services. This increasing demand ultimately stimulates the process of economic development within a region. In the Census of 1981 the work force was classified under three categories, i.e. (i) Main workers, if a worker, works for the major part of the year, (ii) marginal worker if he was worked for less than six months, and (iii) Non-worker if he does not participate in any economically productive work. Usually the age group between 15-59 is considered to be the working age group. On the basis of economic activity the work force of the state has been divisible into several categories which have been given in Table 6.6.

**Table 6.6**
**Jammu and Kashmir State**
**Classification of Workers-1981**

| Cultivators | Agricultural Labourers | Household industry manufacturing, processing services & repairs | Other workers | Total Main workers | Marginal workers | Non-workers |
|---|---|---|---|---|---|---|
| **Rural** | | | | | | |
| 1004340 | 63540 | 96332 | 624802 | 1818571 | 831473 | 3337345 |

| | | | | | | |
|---|---|---|---|---|---|---|
| **Urban** | | | | | | |
| 29557 | 54976 | 64862 | 329862 | 1454040 | 801927 | 2471019 |
| **Total** | | | | | | |
| 10033897 | 63540 | 96332 | 62802 | 1818571 | 831473 | 333745 |

**Source:** Census of India, 1981.

An examination of Table 6.6 shows that in absolute terms there were 18,15,571 main workers and 33,37,345 non-workers in the state, while 8,31,473 are marginal workers in 1981.

It may also be noted from this table that most of the workers are engaged in cultivation of crops, while the household industry and services are providing employment to very little proportion of the workforce. The over-dependence on primary sector in state shows a stage of lope sided development.

The workforce of the state has also been classified on the basis of the National Industrial Classification which has been given in Table 6.7.

In the state cultivators constitute 64.8% of the work force, while 3.1% are agricultural labourers. Nearly 4% is engaged in other primary activities i.e. livestock, forestry, hunting, plantation, orchards, mining, quarrying and allied activities. A little over 2% are dependent on construction while 7.7% are engaged in trade, commerce, transport, communication and storage activities. Other services provide employment to 11.6% of the total work force.

On the whole the state is in the intial stage of development and the work force is largely dependent on primary sector. There is an urgent need to develop industries so that the pressure on primary sector may be reduced. In fact, the development of industrial sector shall stimulate employment and thus will be a permanent source of income. For the development of industry a sound industrial policy needs to be evolved.

**Table 6.7**
**Jammu and Kashmir State**
**Classification of Workers-2001**

| S.No. | Category of workers | Percentage |
|---|---|---|
| I | Cultivators | 64.8 |
| II | Agricultural Labourers | 3.1 |
| III | Livestock, forestry, hunting, plantation orchards and allied activities | 3.7 |
| IV | Mining and quarrying | 0.1 |
| V | Manufacturing, processing, service and repairs (household and others) | 6.7 |
| VI | Construction | 2.3 |
| VII | Trade and commerce | 4.4 |
| VIII | Transport, storage and communication | 3.3 |
| IX | Other services | 11.6 |
| | Total | 100.00 |

**Source:** Digest of Statistics J & K, 2001.

The establishment of agro-based and small scale industries in the different parts can go a long way in giving the state a sound start in industrial development. Tourism can enhance the income of the state and the people substantially and therefore should be a priority sector for development.

## Urbanization

Urbanization is characterized by movements of people from small communities concerned chiefly or solely with agriculture to other communities, generally larger, whose activities are primarily centered in government, trade, manufacturing or allied interests.

Urbanization is both a consequence and a casual factor in economic development. The rate of urban growth is an important indicator of the progress of the economy. In the following paras, urbanization in the State of Jammu and Kashmir has been described briefly.

The State of Jammu and Kashmir has 75.12% of its total population in villages and only 24.88% (2001) in the urban areas.

The size of urban towns and the pattern of their spatial distribution reveal a highly ill-balanced picture. There are 31 towns and urban places in the Jammu Division and 23 in Kashmir Division, while Ladakh has only two towns (Leh and Kargil). Jammu Division with 31 towns has only 33.33% of the total urban population while the 23 towns of Kashmir Division have 65.70% of the total urban population of the state. In Ladakh only 0.97% of the total population is urban (Table 6.8).

## Urban Places of Jammu Division

The towns and urban places of Jammu Division are located mainly in the Jammu plains and on the slopes of the hills. Most of the towns are situated along the National Highway or along the rivers. Jammu, Udhampur, Kathua, Ramban, Ramsu, Batote, Banihal, Rajouri are the examples of such towns. The towns situated along Jammu-Srinagar National Highway are showing steady growth. Contrary to this the towns which have poor connectivity are having stunted growth. The towns of Doda, Kishtwar, Bhadarwah, Karnah, Poonch are showing stagnant growth. Another characterisitc of the Jammu urban population is that over 53% of the total urban population resides in the Jammu Urban Agglomeration. Rajouri and Poonch are the least urbanized districts of the Division. The low level of urbanization of these districts may be attributed to their geo-political location which is not conducive for heavy investment in industries and urbanization.

The urban growth pattern of towns of Jammu Divisions has been shown in Table 6.8.

**Table 6.8**
**Jammu and Kashmir State–Urban Places-1995**

| Division | Percentage of urban population | No. of urban places | Names of urban places |
|---|---|---|---|
| Jammu | 33.33 | 31 | Akhnoor, Arnia, Banihal, Baribrahmani, Basohli, Batote, Bhadarwah, Billawah, Bishna,Chenani, Doda, Hiranagar, Jammu* Kathua, Katra, Kishtwar, Lakhanpur, Nowshera, Parole, Poonch, Ramban, Ramnagar, Ranbirsinghpura, Rajouri, Riasi, Ratanbal, Samba, Thanamandi, Udhampur, Vijaipur. |
| Kashmir | 65.70 | 23 | Achabal, Anantnag, Badgam, Bandipore, Baramulla, Bijbahera, Charisharif, Ganderbal, Gulmarg, Handwara, Kukarnag, Kupwara, Mattan, Pahalgam, Pampore, Pattan, Pulwama, Qazigund Shopian, Sopore, Srinagar*, Tral, Uri. |
| Ladakh | 0.97 | 2 | Kargil, Leh |

**Source:** Census of India, 2001.

* The Urban Agglomeration of Srinagar includes Srinagar City and Badamibagh Contonment, while the Jammu Urban Agglomeration includes Jammu City and Jammu Cantonment.

So far as the decadal growth of urban centres is concerned there was only one town (Jammu) in the region in 1901. Between 1911-12, there had been slower growth. It was after 1931 that a steady increase in the urban places was recorded.

In 1981, sixteen urban hamlets, nine urban villages, three small towns, two medium towns and one city was recorded (Table 6.9). The major occupation of the urban population is trade, commerce, transport, communication, services and manufacturing activities.

**Table 6.9**
**Jammu Division–Urbanization Trend**

| Size and Class | 1901 | 1911 | 1921 | 1931 | 1941 | 1951 | 1961 | 1971 | 1981 |
|---|---|---|---|---|---|---|---|---|---|
| City (10,000 or above | – | – | – | – | – | – | 1 | 1 | 1 |
| Large Towns (50,000–99,999) | – | – | – | – | 1 | 1 | – | – | – |
| Medium Towns (20,000–49,999 | 1 | 1 | 1 | 1 | – | – | – | – | 2 |
| Small Towns (10,000 –19,999) | – | – | – | – | – | – | – | 2 | 3 |
| Urban Village (5,000–9,999) | – | 2 | 2 | 2 | 2 | 2 | 1 | 7 | 9 |
| Urban Hamlets Below 5,000 | – | 15 | 10 | 11 | 11 | 11 | 19 | 14 | 16 |
| Total | 1 | 18 | 13 | 14 | 14 | 14 | 21 | 24 | 31 |

**Source:** Data computed from the Census of India, 1981.

## Urban Places of Kashmir Division

In Kashmir Division there are 23 urban places. Most of these urban places are situated in the plains of Jhelum, *Karewas* and the *Kandi tracts*. Srinagar district has the largest urban population and the district of Kupwara the lowest. Moreover, Srinagar City alone has 73.18% of the total urban population of the Division. Between 1901 and 1921 there had been a sluggish growth of urban places in the Division but after 1921 the towns grew steadily, while the Post-

Independence period recorded a rapid growth in the urban population (Table 6.10).

A comprehensive picture of decadal growth of urban places has been given in Table 6.8. This Table reveals that in 1901 there was only one town (Srinagar) while in 1981 the urban places grew to 23. At the time of the Census 1981 there were seven hamlets, nine urban villages, three small towns, three medium sized towns, no large town (population 50,000–1,00,000) and only one city (Srinagar).

A peculiar feature of urban population of the Kashmir Division is that in ten places (Bandipore, Handwara, Kukarnag Kulgam, Mattan, Pahalgam, Pampore, Sopore, Tral and Uri) most of the people are engaged in primary occupations (agriculture and forestry). In the remaining places industrial activities and services out number the primary activities.

### Ladakh Division

In Ladakh Division there are only two urban places, namely, Kargil and Leh. It is interesting to note that about 45% of the total population of Kargil and Leh towns is dependent on primary activities, about 16% work in transport, 31% in services, 6% in construction and only 3% is engaged in manufacturing.

**Table 6.10**
**Kashmir Division–Urbanization Trend**

| Size and Class | 1901 | 1911 | 1921 | 1931 | 1941 | 1951 | 1961 | 1971 | 1981 |
|---|---|---|---|---|---|---|---|---|---|
| City (over 1,00,000) | 1 | 1 | 1 | 1 | 1 | 1 | 1 | 1 | 1 |
| Large Towns (5,000–99,999) | – | – | – | – | – | – | – | – | – |
| Medium Towns (20,000–49,999) | – | – | – | – | – | – | – | – | – |

| | | | | | | | | | |
|---|---|---|---|---|---|---|---|---|---|
| Small Towns (10,000 –19,999) | – | – | – | 2 | 3 | 3 | 2 | – | 3 |
| Urban Village (5,000–99,999) | – | 3 | 3 | 1 | – | 3 | 3 | 7 | 9 |
| Urban Hamlets Below 5,000 | – | 3 | 3 | 1 | – | 3 | 3 | 7 | 9 |
| Total | 1 | 12 | 7 | 9 | 9 | 8 | 12 | 16 | 23 |

**Source:** Computed from the Census of India, 1901-1981.

### *References*

1. *Census of India* 1971, 2001.
2. *National Council of Applied Economics Research*, 1969, Technoeconomic Survey of J & K, New Delhi.
3. *Gazetteer of Kashmir and Ladakh*, 1974.
4. *Census of India 1981*, Series 8-J & K, Provisional Population Tables.
5. B. Zutshi, 1985, '*Population Distribution of Jammu and Kashmir-A Regional Analysis*' in '*Geography of Jammu and Kashmir*' edt. M. Husain, et. al. New Delhi, pp. 199-213.
6. M. Siddique, 1985, '*Urbanization in Jammu & Kashmir-A Regional Analysis*' in '*Geography of Jammu & Kashmir*' edt. M. Husain, et.al. New Delhi, pp. 215-238.
7. S.N. Agarwala, 1972, '*India's Population Problem*', Delhi.

# PART - III

# ECONOMY

Chapter-VII

# Irrigation and Power Projects

Irrigation has been defined as the distribution of water to land by artificial means in order to enable or enhance the growth of crops. This artificial water may be supplied by canals, wells, tube-wells, tanks etc.

The sub-tropical and temperate latitudes in which the State of Jammu and Kashmir is situated, experience the extremes of weather and climate (Chapter 2). The scorching heat in summer in the Jammu plains, the erratic behaviour of summer monsoon in the Valley of Kashmir and the arid conditions of Ladakh force the farmers to irrigate their crops, wherever sources of irrigation are available. As a matter of fact, in Ladakh crops are grown during summers in small alluvial tracts only with the help of irrigation.

Irrigation, the process of artificial supply of water to crops is an age old practice in the state. The farmers are conscious of the importance of irrigation as a means to achieve an effective breakthrough in the development of agriculture. It is reflected in the eagerness with which some of the Khuls (canals) were constructed by the farmers in the past. After Independence, several irrigation projects were envisaged and completed as a result of which the area under irrigation has increased significantly. The area irrigated in the three Divisions of the state has been given in Table 7.1.

It may be seen from Table 7.1 that about 40.53% of the total cropped area of the state is irrigated. In Ladakh the entire cropped area (19,000 hectares) is dependant on irrigation, while in Jammu and Kashmir Divisions 25% and 61% of the total cropped area is irrigated respectively.

**Table 7.1**
**Jammu & Kashmir State–Irrigated Area–1984-85**
*Area in thousand hectares*

| Division | Total Cropped Area | Area Irrigated | Percentage to Total Cropped Area |
|---|---|---|---|
| Jammu | 576 | 144 | 25.00 |
| Kashmir | 381 | 233 | 61.15 |
| Ladakh | 19 | 19 | 100.00 |
| Total | 976 | 396 | 40.53 |

**Source:** Digest of Statistics, J & K, 1984-85.

The decadal growth in the sources of irrigated and the total area irrigated by each source has been given in Table 7.2.

Statistics about the area irrigated and the source of irrigation given in Table 7.2 show that canals are the dominant source of irrigation in the state. In fact, canals irrigate 305 thousand hectares out of the 324 thousand hectares of irrigated land. The share of canals in irrigation as per the statistics of 1984-85 is over 94 percent.

**Table 7.2**
**Jammu and Kashmir State–Area irrigated (00ha.)**

| Year | Canals | Wells/ Tubewells | Tanks | Other Sources | Total |
|---|---|---|---|---|---|
| 1950–51 | 244.00 | 3.00 | 3.00 | 11.00 | 261.00 |
| 1960–61 | 256.00 | 5.00 | – | 13.00 | 274.00 |
| 1970–71 | 271.00 | 1.00 | 2.00 | 9.00 | 283.00 |
| 1980–81 | 285.00 | 2.00 | 4.00 | 13.00 | 304.00 |
| 1984–85 | 305.00 | 3.50 | 3.10 | 12.40 | 324.00 |

**Source:** Digest of Statistics, Table 4, J & K, State, 1984.

So far as the extension in the sources of irrigation is

concerned in 1950-51 the total irrigated areas was 261 thousand hectares which in 1984-85 increased to 324 thousand hectares, recording an increase of 24%. The mountainous topography and non-availability of underground water in many of the fertile agricultural tracts are the major obstacles in the development of canals and tubewells in the state.

The districtwise area irrigated by canals has been given in Table 7.3 to ascertain the intensity of canal irrigation in the different districts of the state.

**Table 7.3**
**Jammu & Kashmir State–District wise Irrigation (000 hectares)**

| District | Total area irrigated | Area irrigated by canals | Percentage |
|---|---|---|---|
| 1. Anantnag | 47.30 | 46.59 | 98.50 |
| 2. Pulwama | 37.37 | 36.27 | 97.05 |
| 3. Srinagar | 19.26 | 18.26 | 94.80 |
| 4. Badgam | 34.09 | 33.64 | 98.68 |
| 5. Baramulla | 44.71 | 41.61 | 93.07 |
| 6. Kupwara | 22.87 | 21.22 | 92.79 |
| 7. Leh | 9.99 | 9.99 | 100.00 |
| 8. Kargil | 8.75 | 8.75 | 100.00 |
| 9. Jammu | 59.00 | 55.85 | 94.66 |
| 10. Udhampur | 6.00 | 4.83 | 80.50 |
| 11. Doda | 6.68 | 6.46 | 96.71 |
| 12. Kathua | 19.18 | 15.58 | 81.23 |
| 13. Rajouri | 4.91 | 2.35 | 47.86 |
| 14. Poonch | 3.89 | 3.36 | 86.37 |
| Total | 324.00 | 305.00 | 94.14 |

**Source:** Digest of Statistics, J & K, 1984.

The overwhelming dominance of canal irrigation may be seen from the fact that in ten out of the fourteen districts of the state, canals irrigate 92% to 99% of the total irrigated area. The districts of Anantnag, Badgam, Srinagar, Pulwama, Baramulla and Kupwara of the Kashmir Division and Jammu and Doda Districts of Jammu Division have elaborate canal networks and over $9/10^{th}$ of their irrigated area is under the command of canals.

In the state there are several networks of canals constructed by *Zamindars* (Landlords and farmers). A brief description of the major canals of the state is given in the following paras.

**Kashmir Divisions**

The Valley of Kashmir is drained by the Jhelum and its tributaries. Descending from the surrounding mountains the river of Jhelum and its tributaries flow through the *Karewas* and the levelled plains of the valley. The most notable use of the water potential of Jhelum in the valley bottom is for irrigation.

In the Division of Kashmir canals constitute the dominant source of irrigation. These canals are divisible into : (i) the *Zamindari*-canals (*Khul*), and (ii) the Government constructed canals. The *Zamindari* canals, locally known as *Khuls* are constructed and maintained by the farmers. The total number of such canals is 2827 which irrigate nearly 61.15% of the total irrigated area of the Kashmir Valley. Out of these 2827 *Khuls* 259 have been taken over for maintenance by the State Irrigation Department. The major state owned canals are : (i) Martand and (ii) Zainagir.

*(i) The Martand Canals* – This is one of the oldest canals of the state. It is said that it was originally constructed in the $8^{th}$ century A.D. by the king Lalitaditya which got extended by the subsequent rulers. It has been taken off from the left bank of the Lidder river and its Headworks lie at Ganeshpur. The total length of the canal is about 50kms. and it has 9,500 acres of land under its command. The low lying and plain areas of the Anantnag District are irrigated by Martand Canal. The canal terminates in the *Karewa* of Martand and most probably its name has been derived from the Karewa through which it flows and terminates.

*(ii) The Zainagir Canal* – In the $15^{th}$ century A.D., the Zainagir

canal was constructed by Sultan Zain-ul-Abidin. This canal has been excavated from the Madhumati river (a left hand tributary of Jhelum). The canal has been constructed along the northern side of the Wular-Lake through Sopore and Zainagir. It provides water to the paddy fields and orchards of Baramulla District and has about 13,300 acres of area under its command.

The network of *Khuls* is quite dense which gives the impression of a labyrinth (Fig. 14). Some of the important *Khuls* of Kashmir are Sharakhul, Shahkhul, Sumbal, Nandi, Zainpur, Awantipore, Kayal, Rishipura and Babul. At the occurrence of water scarcity, the villagers regulate the supply through *Rahviks* (watchmen). The *Rahviks* Committee is formed by the villagers.

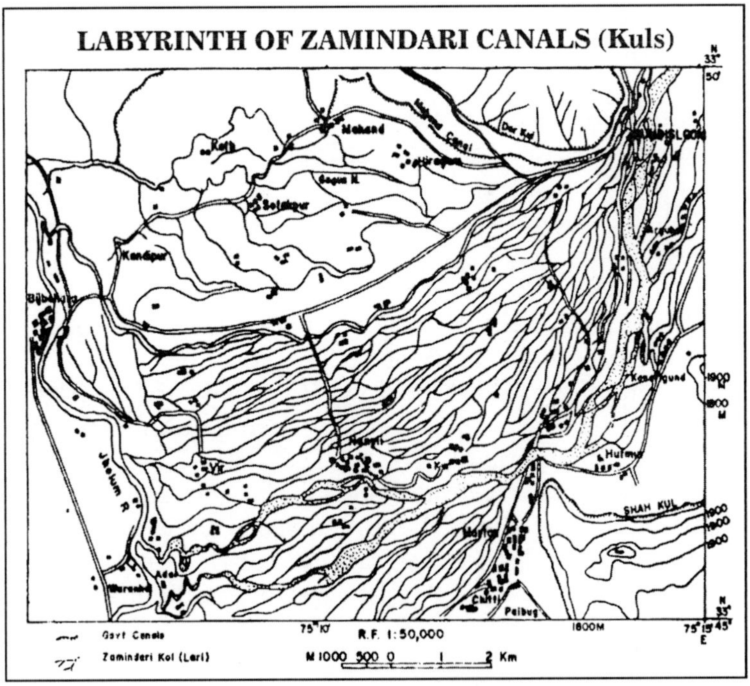


**Fig. 14 : Labyrinth of Zamindari Canals (Kuls)**

Throughout the history, the *Zamindari* canals have been of immense assistance in saving the crops and are still useful providing water to the crops. But after the abolition of *Zamindari*-System many of them have not been properly maintained. Such canals which have been ignored are proving to be a menace to the adjoining agricultural areas. At the occurrence of heavy rains and melting of snow, they spill over and submerge the adjacent fields, many times causing serious damage to standing crops. Recently, a comprehensive plan has been prepared for their restoration and maintenance. Efforts however, need to be made to extend these canals in the dry farming areas, especially in those *Karewas* which are devoted to maize cultivation. Such *Karewas*, if provided with irrigation may be used for the cultivation of more valuable crops, like paddy, oilseeds and orchards.

### Jammu Division

The Division of Jammu is drained by the Chenab, Ravi, Tawi, Ujh, Basantar, Manawar Tawi, Poonch Tohi and Neru rivers. Many of these are hill torrents and discharge little quantities of water during the summer and winter seasons. Wherever possible, the water of these rivers has been utilized for irrigation. Some of the important canals of Jammu Division have been described briefly in the following paras:

### The Ranbir Singh Canal

The Headworks of Ranbir Singh Canal is located at Akhtoor on the left bank of Chenab. Passing southward it has been taken across the Tawi River with the help of an aquaduct. The fertile plains of Jammu and Ranbirsinghpura are under its command. The total command area of Ranbir Singh Canal is over one lakh acres. This canal and its distributers have helped appreciably in the adoption and diffusion of High Yielding Varieties of rice and wheat in Jammu plain, especially in the tehsil of Ranbirsinghpura.

### The Pratap Canal

Taken out from the right bank of the mighty Chenab, at Akhnoor, the Chenab canal has a total length of 36kms. About 20,000 acres of Akhnoor Tehsil are under its command. Rice, wheat, oilseeds, fodder and vegetables are the major crops irrigated by Pratap Canal.

### The Ravi-Tawi Irrigation Complex

A comprehensive project has been designed to connect the Ravi and Tawi waters for irrigation purposes. On completion this project will irrigate about one and a half lakh acres of land in the *Kandi* and plain areas of the Jammu Division. The complex is based on the gravity canals and lift irrigation projects which is expected to cost about Rs. 70 crores. The project consists of : (a) the Ravi Canal, and (b) the Tawi Lift Irrigation Project.

#### (a) The Ravi Canal

The Ravi Canal has been taken out from the right bank of the Ravi River at the Shahpur-Kandi Barrage. Moving in a north-east to south-west direction, the main canal is 76kms. long. It has been linked with the Tawi Lift Project at Vijaipur. Efforts are being made to transfer the water of Kathua Canal into Ravi Canal at Lakhanupur. In its middle course a 356m. long barrage is to be constructed on the Ujh River and the main canal. After completion the project will assure cultivation of High Yielding Varieties of rice and wheat in the Jammu and Kathua Tehsils.

#### (b) The Tawi Lift Irrigation Project

A lift station has been constructed on the left bank of the Tawi River near Bahu-Fort. At this point the water of Tawi River is raised to height of about 31 metres by lift pumps and fed into the main canal. The main canal has a length of about 29km. which has been constructed from Jammu to Ramgarh. It commands about 15,000 acres of the Jammu, Bishna and Vijaipur Blocks.

In the southern plains of Jammu a number of tubewells operated by the diesel pumps or hydel power have been installed. About 2100 hectares of arable land are irrigated by tubewells in the Jammu Division.

## Ladakh Division

Owing to scanty rains and high rate of evaporation the cultivation of crops in the Ladakh Division is entirely dependent on irrigation. Many of the farmers have individual water channels to irrigate their fields. Moreover, there are several small canals locally known as *Mayur* which irrigate relatively larger tracts of cultivated land.

*(i) The Chuchot Mayur (Canal)*

The Chuchot-Mayur has been taken out of the left bank of the Indus at the Stakna. It commands about 200 acres of Chuchot, Gongma, Shama, Yokam and Balam villages. Wheat, *grim* (a type of barley) and vegetables are the main crops irrigated by the Chuchot-Mayur.

*(ii) The Thiksay Mayur (Canal)*

The Thiksay Mayur has been dug from the right bank of the Indus river. It provides water to the village of Ranbirpora, situated on a low terrace of Indus. About 120 acres of cultivated area of Ranbirpora is under the command of Thiksay Canal.

## Tank Irrigation

Nearly 3100 hectares of arable land of the state are under tank irrigation. Tank irrigation is confined to isolated tracts in the districts of Anantnag, Pulwama, Srinagar, Badgam and Kupwara. Tank irrigation is however, insignificant in the Jammu Division as only 90 hectares are irrigated by tanks in Poonch District.

Rice and wheat are the dominant crops irrigated. Rice along constitutes over 60% of the total irrigated area, followed by wheat which covers about 13% of the gross irrigated area. Maize, pulses, oilseeds, millets, orchards and vegetables are the other crops irrigated in the state.

Table 7.4
Jammu & Kashmir State–Crops Irrigated 1983-84

| Crop | Area in hectares | Percentage |
|---|---|---|
| 1. Rice | 2,45,000 | 60.49 |
| 2. Maize | 16,000 | 3.95 |
| 3. Wheat | 52,000 | 12.84 |
| 4. Pulses & Millets | 16,000 | 3.95 |
| 5. Other food crops | 21,000 | 5.19 |
| 6. Other non-food crops | 55,000 | 13.58 |
| Total | 4,05,000 | 100.00 |

**Source:** Computed from the Digest of Statistics, J & K Govt.

## Power Development, Consumption and Potential

Power is the key to high level of economic development. Its level of consumption in any country is a significant indicator of development. As for instance, U.S.A. which is economically one of the most developed countries claims a per capita consumption of 8487 units per day. In sharp contrast is the Indian average per capita consumption of 133 units. In the State of Jammu and Kashmir it is even much less with only 93 units per capita per day. This state is among the most under developed states of India and will continue to stay in this state of backwardness unless adequate steps are taken to improve its power situation. The state is poor in coal (Chapter 4) and because of the unfavourable geological structure, the prospects of striking gas and petroleum are not very promising. It has however, tremendous potential for hydro-electricity generation which has been taped inadequately. In the following paras the water power development has been described.

## Hydel Power

The three mighty rivers viz. Indus, Jhelum and Chenab and their numerous perennial tributaries which drain the state provide immense opportunities for the generation of hydroelectricity. It has been estimated that these rivers provide theoretically a potential of 13,000 MW of hydel power generation. The major hydel projects, their installed and effective capacities have been given in Table 7.5.

The electric power available from the above sources is 956 MUs per year which is inadequate to meet the present demands of primary, secondary and tertiary sectors.

The state is connected to the Northern Grid by two 220 KV A/C Lines. One between Sarna and Udhampur and the other between Sarna and Gladni to be extended to Salal Hydro-Electric Project (HEP). These two lines have a carrying capacity of 243 MWs only. Further the regions of Jammu and Kashmir are connected by a D/C 132 KV line between Udhampur and Bemina. The NHPC is also constructing one more D/C 400 KV Line between Udhampur and Srinagar which was expected to be complete by the end of the VIII Fiver Year Plan.

**Potential Hydel Power**

*Ladakh Division :*

The Kargil and Leh Districts of Ladakh Division are traversed by the Indus and its tributaries (Shyok, Zanskar, Suru). The main Indus River drains the range between Ladakh and Karakoram. Its catchment at Karu is 3840 sq. kms.

On the basis of meagre data available about the Indus river, it is estimated that this river has an annual flow of about 13 lakh cubic ft. Although data on the discharge of Zanskar is not available, it appears that its annual discharge at Nimu (Leh District) would be more then that of Indus at Leh. The Shyok River has a similar pattern of discharge. All these rivers have a steep gradient descending from a height of about 4,300 metres to about 2,500 metres. The annual flow of these rivers gives a mean discharge of 9,500 cusecs which may generate 3,000 MW/years. This hydel potential is to be harnessed for a rapid development of Ladakh Division.

*Kashmir Division:*

The outflow of the Jhelum river drainage Kashmir Valley

**Table 7.5**
**Status of Electric Power in Jammu & Kashmir State-1985**

| Division | Project | Installed capacity | Effective capacity MW Summer | Winter |
|---|---|---|---|---|
| A-Jammu | (i) Chenani | 25 | 20 | 12 |
| | (ii) Kalakote (Thermal) | 21.4 | – | 4 |
| | (iii) Other small stations | 3.0 | 2 | 17 |
| B-Kashmir | (iv) L. Jhelum H.P. | 105 | 105 | 65 |
| | (v) U. Jhelum Stage I. | 22.6 | 22 | 17 |
| | (vi) Ganderbal | 15.0 | 12 | 10.5 |
| | (vii) Mohra | 9 | 7 | 7 |
| | (viii) Bemina and others | 6 | – | 4.5 |
| C-Imports | State Share from B.B.M. | – | 27 | 27 |
| | Grand Total | 208.1 | | |

**Source:** Energy Planning Wing, Govt. of Jammu & Kashmir.

at Baramulla is of the order of 9,000 cusecs. Moreover, the Kishan-Ganga which drains the northern slopes of Dholadhar Mountain and Southern slope of Nanga Parbat brings an additional flow of 1,290 cusecs. Most of this water reaches in it from about 3,500 metres to 1,200 metres. The Jhelum River as such has theoretical hydel potential of 3,000 MW/year. Work on various projects is under progress. The completion of the Uri-Project will ease the electricity shortages appreciably, and therefore deserves special attention of the government.

*Jammu Division:*

Traversed by the mighty Chenab, Jammu Division is more richly endowed in hydel energy potential that other parts of the state. Theoretically this river has hydel potential of about 500 MW/years. The completion of Salal and Dul-Hasti Projects will go a long way in overcoming the deficiency of electricity in the state.

***References***

1. R.O. Buchanan, 1974, '*An Illustrated Dictionary of Geography*', Mc Graw-Hill, Singapore.
2. Govt. of India, '*Irrigation and Power Projects*', Ministry of Irrigation and Power, New Delhi-1970.
3. Govt. of India, '*Irrigation Atlas of India*', Ministry of Irrigation and Power, New Delhi-1970.
4. Govt. of J & K, *Digest of Statistics*, 1984.
5. A.K. Koul, '*Home Geography*', 1985.
6. S.M. Alam, M. Husain, 1986, '*Energy Scenario in the State of Jammu and Kashmir*', TERI Publication.

Chapter-VIII

# Agriculture

The domestication of plants and animals is know as agriculture. Still most of the population of the world is dependent on agriculture. Consequently, the productive plains are the areas of high concentration of population and the State of Jammu and Kashmir is no exception to this. The outer plains of Jammu and the fertile Valley of Kashmir are intensively cultivated while the dry plateau of Ladakh and lofty mountainous areas of Jammu and Kashmir are almost uncultivated.

Cultivation of crops is the dominant occupation in Jammu and Kashmir. Farming, directly or indirectly supports about 81% of the total population of the State. While 70% of the workforce is engaged in agriculture. It contributes nearly 60% of the state revenue which adequately explains the over dependence of the state on agriculture.

**Land Use**

The total area of the state is 2.23 lakh sq. kms. out of which about 1.39 lakh sq.kms. is on this side of the Line of Actual Control. About 92% of the geographical area of the state consists of high mountains and only about 5% is available for cultivation. A general picture of land use of the state has been given in Table 8.1.

An analysis to Table 8.1 shows that a little over 27% of the total area of the state is under forest and about 30% is available for cultivation. Permanent pastures and culturable waste cover 5.17% and 5.84% of the area respectively, while about 12% is put to non-agricultural uses. A little over 12% is barren land. The forest area is however, shrinking at a faster pace which in several districts of the valley (Pulwama, Badgam and Srinagar) has reached the critical limit of ecological equilibrium.

**Table 8.1**
**Jammu and Kashmir–General Land Use–1999-2000**
**Area in-000 hectares**

| Use of Land | Area in thousand hectares | Percentage of total area of the State |
|---|---|---|
| 1. Forest | 658 | 27.24 |
| 2. Net area sown | 730 | 30.22 |
| 3. Land put to non-agricultural uses | 291 | 12.04 |
| 4. Barren land | 293 | 12.13 |
| 5. Permanent pastures and other grazing grounds | 125 | 5.17 |
| 6. Land under Misc. trees and other groves | 72 | 2.98 |
| 7. Culturable waste | 141 | 5.84 |
| 8. Fallow other than current fallow | 7 | 0.29 |
| 9. Current fallow | 99 | 4.00 |
| Total | 2416 | 100.00 |

**Source:** Revenue Deptt. J & K, Srinagar.

## Cropping Patterns

Cropping pattern has been defined as the proportion of area under various crops at a point of time. The statistics of crops are used to denote cropping patterns. It is, however, a dynamic concept which changes in space and time. In fact, no cropping pattern can be good and ideal for all times to come.

The state of Jammu and Kashmir has micro level variations in agro-climatic conditions. Consequently, the cropping patterns and crop combinations differ significantly at the meso and micro levels. The Jammu plains landscape is dominated by wheat, rice, pulses, maize, oilseeds and fodder, the valley of Kashmir is well known for paddy, maize, saffron and orchards cultivation, while in Ladakh *grim* (a type of barley) and vegetables are the main crops (Table 8.2).

**Table 8.2**
**Jammu & Kashmir State–Area Under Different Crops 1995–96**

| Crop | Area in thousand hectares | Percentage |
|---|---|---|
| 1. Rice | 273.00 | 28.58 |
| 2. Jowar (Millets) | 16.14 | 1.39 |
| 3. Bajra | 13.30 | 2.23 |
| 4. Maize | 305.00 | 31.93 |
| 5. Wheat | 250.00 | 26.17 |
| 6. Barley | 7.68 | 0.80 |
| 7. Pulses | 34.25 | 3.58 |
| 8. Sugarcane | 0.32 | 0.03 |
| 9. Fruits and vegetables | 61.47 | 6.44 |
| 10. Other food crops | 1.85 | 0.19 |
| Total | 955.11 | 100.00 |

**Source:** Digest of Statistics, Govt. of J & K, 1995-96.

By and large the cropping structure of the state shows a subsistence character. Rice, maize and wheat, the three staple food crops of the state occupy over 83% of the gross cropped area. Rice is the leading crop, occupying 28.58% of the cropped land followed by maize and wheat, which are sown in about 31% and 26% of the total cropped area respectively. Millets, *Bajra*, pulses, fodder, orchards and vegetables are the other important crops grown in the state (Table 8.3).

### Table 8.3
### District-wise Distribution of Major Crops-Total Area 912.81 hectares Area in thousand hectares–1982-84

| District | Rice | Wheat | Maize | Pulses | Orchards & Vegetables |
|---|---|---|---|---|---|
| Anantnag | 41.04 | – | 22.02 | 3.45 | 7.03 |
| | 14.89% | | 7.98 | | |
| Pulwama | 30.17 | 0.47 | 112.21 | 2.47 | 11.91 |
| | 10.95% | 0.93% | 4.06% | | |
| Srinagar | 13.80 | 0.07 | 4.56 | 0.52 | 59.8 |
| | 5.00% | 0.03% | 1.65% | | |
| Badgam | 27.51 | 2.37 | 13.24 | 2.36 | 5.34 |
| | 9.98% | 1.14% | 4.80% | | |
| Baramulla | 35.52 | 0.41 | 21.84 | 6.40 | 14.58 |
| | 12.89% | 0.19% | 10.45% | | |
| Kupwara | 17.72 | 0.01 | 20.21 | 1.21 | 4.76 |
| | 6.43% | | 7.32% | | |
| Leh | – | 2.43 | – | 0.36 | 0.31 |
| | | 1.14% | | | |
| Kargil | – | 2.04 | – | 1.07 | 0.12 |
| | | 1.40% | | | |
| Jammu | 54.37% | 90.33 | 11.67 | 11.77 | 2.16 |
| | 19.73% | 42.46% | 4.22% | | |
| Udhampur | 11.98 | 33.14 | 47.52 | 5.63 | 0.28 |
| | 4.35 | 15.51% | 17.21% | | |
| Doda | 3.90 | 7.14 | 40.91 | 3.52 | 0.73 |
| | 1.42% | 3.36% | 14.82% | | |
| Kathua | 28.69 | 41.18 | 15.66 | 6.99 | 0.33 |
| | 10.41 | 19.36% | 5.67% | | |
| Rajouri | 6.78 | 24.68 | 31.28 | 1.95 | 0.02 |
| | 2.46% | 11.60% | 13.86% | | |
| Poonch | 4.13 | 7.96 | 21.96 | 0.15 | 0.07 |
| | 1.50% | 3.74% | 7.95% | | |
| Total | 215.61 | 212.73 | 276.07 | 47.60 | 53.62 |
| | 100% | 100% | 100% | | |

**Source:** Computed from the data, Digest of Statistics, J & K, 1983-84

A districtwise analysis of area under different crops shows

that rice dominates in Jammu, Anantnag, Baramulla, Pulwama, Kathua and Badgam. In each of these districts at least 10% of the gross cropped area is under paddy cultivation. Its cultivation is altogether absent in Leh, Kargil (Ladakh), while in the remaining districts it occupies less than 6% of the cropped area.

So far as the distributional pattern of wheat is concerned, its high concentration lies in Jammu (42.46%), Kathua (19.36%), Udhampur (15.58%) and Rajouri (11.60%). In the Valley of Kashmir the process of its diffusion has been started but still none of the districts has even 1% of the cropped area under its cultivation excepting Badgam in which a little over 1% of the gross cropped area is devoted to wheat.

Maize is a significant crop of the state and its major concentration sprawls in the *Kandi* areas. In the districts of Udhampur, Doda and Rajouri its share in the total cropped area is 17%, 14% and 13% respectively. Poonch, Kathua, Jammu, Kupwara, Baramulla, Badgam, Anantnag and Pulwama are the other districts of its high concentration. In the remaining districts (Leh, Kargil and Srinagar) maize is an insignificant crop.

**Rice : *(Oryza Sativa)***

Rice thrives well in the hot and moist climate. In the Valley of Kashmir warm and moist conditions prevail from May to August, and this period records mean monthly temperature over 20°C with adequate rains. The period is thus ideally suited for rice cultivation. Deep fertile clay soils that turn into soft mud when puddled and develop cracks when dry are most considered conducive for the cultivation of rice. Such soils are found in the Jammu Plain and in the Kashmir Valley.

In the Valley of Kashmir rice is generally transplanted in the third week of May, while in the outer plains of Jammu Division its transplantation takes place in the beginning of July after the onset of summer monsoon, and the crop is harvested in September and October. The High Yielding

Varieties (HYV) of rice have been diffused in the areas where controlled irrigation by canals or tubewells is available. In the *Kandi* areas wherever, soils are clayey, rice is grown as a rain – fed crop. The Valley of Kashmir is often been called as the '*Rice Bowl*' of the state, while the Tehsil of Ranbirsinghpura (Jammu) is well known for its good quality of rice.

On the low lands, the preparation of fields for rice cultivation is carried out under the dry and puddled system. the former involves repeated ploughings of fields. It is sown either by broadcast or transplanted. In transplantation, seedling are raised in nurseries and after about forty days are transplanted in the paddy fields.

Though rice is grown in Jammu plains, *Kandi* lands, Udhampur, Bhadarwah region and the Jhelum plains, its major concentration lies in the districts of Jammu, Kupwara, Anantnag, Baramulla, Srinagar, Pulwama and Kathua.

The average yield of paddy varies from region to region and from latitude to altitude. The average yield of rice in Kashmir Division is about 15 quintals per hectare while, in the Jammu Division the average yield per hectare is about 13 quintals. In both the cases it is above the national average of 12 quintals per hectare. There are however, intra-regional variations in the yield of rice. For example, in Ranbirsinghpura the yield of rice per hectare is much higher to that of Udhampur and Bhadarwah Tehsils.

The total production of rice in the state was about 6,000 quintals in 2000-02, out of which nearly 75% was produced in the Kashmir Valley and only 25% in the Jammu Division. The production of rice can be raised substantially, if new High Yielding Varieties are diffused, especially in the areas with controlled supply of irrigation.

**Wheat (*Triticum*)**

Wheat is a staple crop which requires cool and moist weather conditions. At the time of sowing the night temperatures should be about 15°C. It thrives well if the average temperature remains around 18°C. At the time of ripening the day temperatures should be about 30°C. Wheat requires about 30cm. to 50cm. rainfall. At the failure of rains the crop needs to be irrigated repeatedly. Wheat is a *rabi* crop in Jammu and Kashmir Divisions and *kharif* crop in Ladakh Division. In Jammu and Kashmir it is sown, generally, in the month of November and harvested in April. In the Valley of Kashmir, it is sown in October and remains dormant under the low temperatures of winters. The crop shows rapid growth during springs as the temperature starts rising. Well drained loams and clayey loams are considered ideal for wheat cultivation. It requires a well pulverised but compact seed-bed for good germination. The fields are ploughed and pulverised several times before the seed is sown.

Wheat has been diffused in almost all the districts of the state, but its major concentration lies in Jammu (42%), Kathua (19%), Udhampur (16%) and Rajouri (11%). In rest of the districts, the temperatures are not conducive for its cultivation. It is interesting to note that wheat has also been diffused in the Leh and Kargil Districts of Ladakh Division. In Ladakh wheat is a *Kharif* (summer crop) sown in May and harvested in August or September. On the whole, wheat occupies about 26% of the total cropped area of the state.

Wheat cultivation is done in about 2,12,000 hectares out of which 2,04,000 acres are in Kashmir Valley. The Suru Valley of Kargil is coming up as the '*wheat bowl*' of Ladakh.

### Maize *(Zea–Mays)*

Maize is the second important cereal crop of the state occupying nearly 32% of the total cropped area. Maize requires hot and moist climate for its cultivation. The soil should be well drained in which water does not remain standing. During the period of its growth, maize requires several hoeings. At the failure of rains, the crop gives better results only if irrigation is made. The sandy-loam tracts of Jammu plains, the Kandi lands of the state and the *Karewas* (suitable for agriculture but not under saffron or orchards) are generally devoted to maize.

Maize is not only used as a green fodder, it is a staple food for the people who live in the *Kandi* areas, especially the Gujjars of Jammu Division.

Nearly 3,05,000 hectares (32%) out of the 9,13,000 hectares of gross cropped area of the state in 1983-84 was under maize cultivation. Its areal distribution shows that the districts of Udhampur (47%), Doda (41%), Rajouri (38%) and Poonch (22%) are the leading maize producing districts of the Jammu Division, while in the Kashmir Division its main concentration lies in Baramulla (29%), Anantnag (22%) and Kupwara (20%) (Table 8.3).

The total production of maize in 1983-84 was approximately 3821 thousand quintals giving an average yield of about less than 2.5 quintals per acre. The low yield per acre may be attributed to the agro-climatic conditions and the non-availability of High Yielding Variety Seeds of maize.

Among the other cereal and non-cereal crops grown in the state, *Bajra*, pulses (green-gram, black-gram, red-gram), barley, *grim* (a type of barley), millets, oil-seeds and fodder are important.

### Saffron (*Crocus Sativus*)

Saffron is one of the important cash crops of the Jammu and Kashmir state. Its cultivation is carried on in the *Karewas* of Kashmir Valley and Kishtwar (Jammu Division). The cultivation of saffron is closely influenced by the prevailing temperatures, rains, snowfall, soil-texture and the underground watertable.

Persistence of extreme cold and scorching heat are unfavourable where as temperate conditions with light snowing are considered to be conducive for saffron cultivation. Day temperature above 25°C from April to August with occasional showers are required for a good crop. In October and November (flowering period of saffron) the night temperature should be close to the freezing point. Although the plant needs different temperature and moisture conditions in the different parts of the year, long spells of rains and rainless intervals affect the outturn of the crop adversely.

Saffron thrives well in a well-drained *Karewa* soil. The underground waterable should be more than 2.5 metres deep as the high waterable damages the croms of saffron. The lacustrine deposits (*Karewas*), composed of blue, grey and buff silt and sand intermixed with conglomerates and terminal moraines are the ideal pedological conditions for the successful cultivation of saffron.

Apart from agro-climatic conditions, the cultivation of saffron also depends on the economic condition of the farmer. The seeds and labour costs are high and a poor farmer cannot afford these costly inputs. Moreover, in the first two years, there is no return from the saffron field which makes the poor farmer shy in the adoption of its cultivation.

The various operations adopted in its cultivation may be summed up as under. At the advent of spring in April and May the field is repeatedly ploughed either by plough or twice by tractor at an interval of about 20 days. Subsequently, clodding, levelling and hoeing operations are done which continue till the middle of August. In September seed corms are planted in 15-20 cm wide furrows at a depth of about 8 cm. The field after sowing is divided into about 2 metres wide strips. On all sides of these strips about 15 cm deep and 30 cm wide drainage channels are made which resemble to a chess-board. The rectangular seed bed sides are made to drain out the water quickly.

The hoeing of saffron field is done generally twice in June and August. Hoeing is repeated every year till the corm reproduction over conjust the soil after which the field is dishoarded for being prepared for a fresh sowing.

Saffron crop is harvested in the later parts of October and the early parts of November. During the period picking of saffron flowers just after the disappearance of due is imperative to obtain good fragrance. From the flowers stigmas are removed and classified into *Shahi*, *Mongra* and *Laccha* categories of saffron.

Initially, saffron cultivation was confined to the Pampore-*Karewa* but now it has been diffused in the various parts of the valley. Its cultivation is being done in the fourteen tehsils of five districts of the Kashmir Division. It has been diffused in 190 villages of the Kashmir Division. Pulwama Tehsil with 75% of the total saffron area has the largest concentration, while the remaining thirteen tehsils share 25% of the saffron area. There are still many unutilized *Karewas* in which saffron can be diffused provided extension service and subsidy to the farmers are given.

## Horticulture

Horticulture is a type of agriculture in which generally garden crops e.g. fruits, flowers and vegetables are grown. The word is derived from the Latin word Hourtus=garden and Colere=cultivate. The concept of garden culture as a distinct form of field culture dated back to the farming system that used extensive areas for grains, forage, fodder and pastures.

Horticulture is traditionally divided into (i) pomology, e.g. food crops, nuts, vines and (ii) floriculture e.g. edible-roots, edible-stems, edible-leaf, edible-seeds and flowers. The State of Jammu and Kashmir has great diversity in the geo-ecological conditions which ideally suit for the cultivation of almost all kinds of temperate and some varieties of tropical and sub-tropical fruits.

Horticulture is an old economic activity in the state of Jammu and Kashmir. Kalhana, the great Kashmiri historian mentioned fruit culture in Kashmir in his famous book 'Rajtarangini' during the reign of King Nara as back as 1000 B.C. It was however, during the period of Lalitaditya (900 A.D.) that horticulture in the state received considerable patronage. Subsequently, during the periods of Zainul-Abidin and the Mughals some varieties of fruits were brought from Kabul, Persia (Iran) and Central Asia.

At present about 8,10,000 hectares are under orchards in the state. The districtwise distribution of area under orchards has been given in Table 8.4

**Table 8.4**
**Districtwise Distribution of Orchards in 1994-94**
**Total Area 8,10,000 Hectares**

| District | Area in hectares | Percentage |
|---|---|---|
| 1. Srinagar | 28,396 | 3.50 |
| 2. Badgam | 25,332 | 6.83 |
| 3. Anantnag | 76,504 | 9.44 |
| 4. Pulwama | 64,151 | 7.91 |
| 5. Baramulla | 92,581 | 11.30 |
| 6. Kupwara | 45,925 | 5.66 |
| 7. Leh | 9,872 | 1.21 |
| 8. Kargil | 8,630 | 1.06 |
| 9. Jammu | 1,40,480 | 17.34 |
| 10. Udhampur | 74,134 | 9.15 |
| 11. Kathua | 72,922 | 9.00 |
| 12. Doda | 64,686 | 7.98 |
| 13. Rajouri | 50,618 | 6.24 |
| 14. Poonch | 26,778 | 3.38 |

**Source:** Digest of Statistics, 1994-95, J & K State.

An examination of Table 8.4 reveals that fruits, nuts and vegetable are grown in substantial acreage in each districts of the State. Orchards however, have high concentration in Jammu (17.34%), Baramulla (11.3%), Anantnag, Udhampur and Kathua Districts.

The Valley of Kashmir, part of Doda, Kathua, Udhampur, Rajouri and Poonch district fall in temperate zone which is conducive for the cultivation of temperate fruits and nuts. These districts have high acreage under apples, cherry, peach, *Nakh*, plum, grapes, pomegranates, apricot, pears, almond, walnut and chestnut.

9. Picking of Flowers of Saffron-A Pleasant Hobby

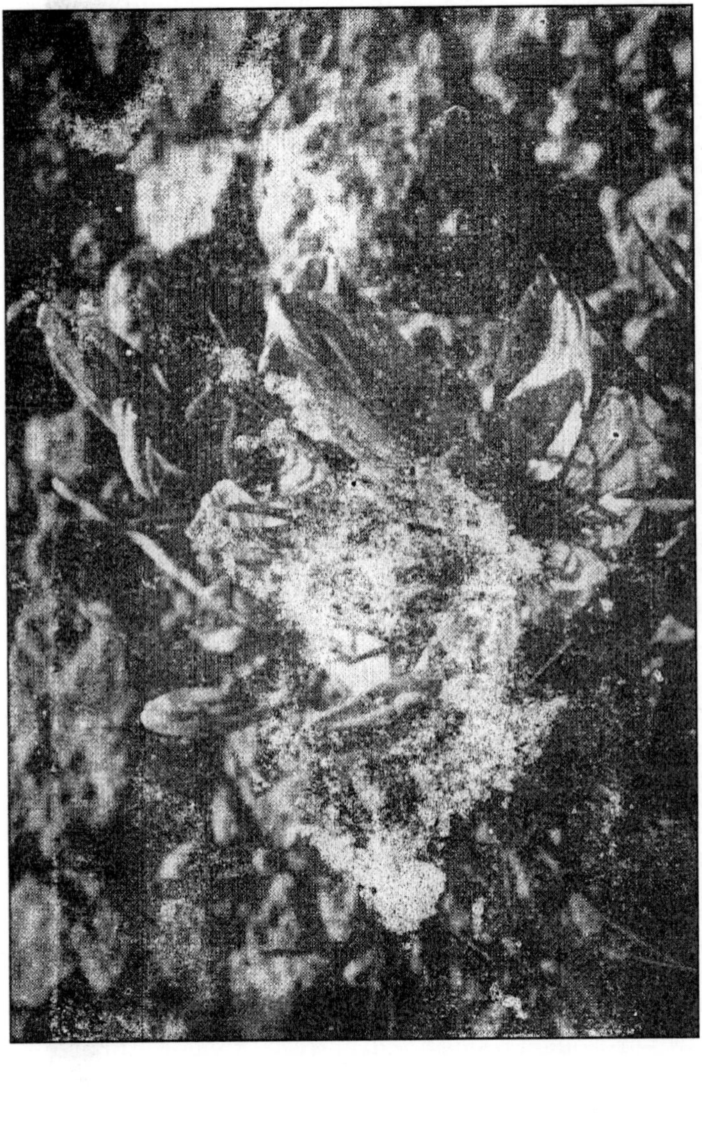

10. Saffron flowers with Stigmas

Most of the apple orchards lie between 1800 and 2750 metres above the sea level. The sandy soil is not suited to the cultivation of apple orchards as they induce root-bores attack and pink disease. Deep and heavy loams are more suitable for orchards which can retain moisture for a longer period. Some of the important varieties of apple grown in the Valley of Kashmir are Ambri, American-Tarel, Delicious, Maharaji, Hazratbali, Kesari and Royal Misri. The districts of Baramulla, Anantnag and Srinagar have over 80% of the total apple orchards of the state.

Pears (*Nakh*) and peach also grow well in the cool and humid climate of the Kashmir Valley. Peach is however, highly perishable and farmers are not much inclind in the expansion of its orchards. Pears and peach orchards are well scattered in the different districts of Kashmir Division.

Apricot (*Khoobani*) fruit requires humid nights, and cool weather during the early parts of its growing period and moderately high (25°C) temperature during later parts of development. Leh and Kargil districts of Ladakh and the hilly areas of Kashmir below 3000 metre are suited for apricot orchards.

In the Jammu Division sub-tropical fruits e.g. mangoes, oranges, maltas, *Ber*, plum, papaya, guava, peach, *Litchi*, lemon and grapes are grown. About 500 varieties of mango, each with a particular taste and flavour are found in the state, especially in the Jammu Division. However, only a few of these are of commercial importance. The crop takes about 4 months (March-June) to mature.

In 1982-83 there were 25 million fruit trees in the state. At present several new projects have been launched to spread orchards in Jammu and Kashmir State. Incentives have been offered by the various departments of the state to develop orchards in drought prone *Kandi* and hilly areas. Fifty percent subsidy on plant material is being provided to the growers of the state. Consequently, more than 5050 acres have been covered under this scheme. For a steady expansion of horticulture, the grower must provide precise inputs and be vigilent against pests and disease. In fact, exact scheduling is imperative since most of the fruits and flower crops are highly perishable. Transportation to market must function smoothly to avoid losses.

Area of fruits like apples, walnut, *Litchi*, pear, cherries and apricot have increased since 1980, while the area of almond, *Lauqat* and peaches is shrinking.

From the state nearly 37.5 lakh tonnes of fruits are exported annually. Besides, Delhi, Mumbai, Chennai (Madras), Hyderabad and Banglore, the fruits (fresh and dry) and nuts are exported to the various towns and cities of Punjab, Haryana, Uttar Pradesh, Bihar, Madhya Pradesh, Rajasthan and Andhra Pradesh.

One of the main hindrances in the development and expansion of orchards is the marketing of fruits. The packing and transportation costs are substantially high and the orchard farming is facing a tough competition from other states. Moreover, the packing of fruits in wooden boxes in consuming enormous quantities of soft and superior timber. These problems may be overcome if fruit canning industries could be established at suitable places in the state.

## Sericulture

The rearing of silk worms on mulberry trees for the production of raw-silk is known as sericulture. In the state, mulberry trees in the wild form existed from antiquity. In Kashmiri language the silk-fibre is known as '*Pote*' and the silk-worm is the Patikeom (insects). *Pote* manufacturing in the valley is an old industry. Sericulture involves the stages, of:

(i) Rearing of silk worm;
(ii) Collection of cocoons and their delivery for reeling purpose;
(iii) Reeling of raw silk from the cocoons; and
(iv) Availability of mulberry trees from which fresh leaves (the feed of silk worms) can be obtained.

11. Harvested Saffron Flowers

Rearing of silk worm requires scientific knowledge technical skill. For the development of healthy silk worm two basic seed station have been established at Udhampur and Miragund. Work on the Qazigund Nursery is also under progress. There are 2,800 villages and 33,000 households in which sericulture has become an important economic activity. Out of these 1500 villages are situated in the Kashmir Division and the remaining 1300 villages in the Jammu Division. The areal sprawl and production pattern in the State has been given in Table 8.5.

**Table 8.5**
**Sericulture in Jammu & Kashmir State–1999-2000**

| | | Kashmir Division Quantity | Kashmir Division No/ percent | Jammu Division Quantity | Jammu Division No/ percent | Total |
|---|---|---|---|---|---|---|
| 1. | Mulberry trees | 30,200 | 47.41 | 3,35,000 | 52.59 | 6,37,000 |
| 2. | No. of Sericulture Villages | 15,000 | 53.57 | 13,000 | 46.62 | 28,000 |
| 3. | No. of Sericulture households | 12,300 | 37.217 | 20,700 | 62.73 | 33,000 |
| 4. | Production of Cocoons | 4,430 | 66.32 | 2,250 | 62.73 | 6,680 |
| 5. | Production of raw silk in quantity | 35,800 | 82.36 | 7,670 | 17.64 | 43,470 qtls. |
| | in value of lakh Rs. | 1,82,010 | 77.85 | 5,12.800 | 22.15 | 2382\10 |

**Source:** Digest of Statistics, J & K, Srinagar.

In the state there are about 6.37 lakh mulberry trees, out of which 53% (3,35,000) are in Jammu Division and 47% in Kashmir Division. Annually about 6,680 quintals of raw silk is produced which is approximately equivalent to Rs. 50 million.

Inadequacy of mulberry leaves and damage caused by insects and pests are the major problems in the development and expansion of mulberry trees. Now the Sericulture

Development Department is laying stress on raising dwarf mulberry trees to supplement and replenish the traditional tall mulberry trees. As a result of these efforts the dwarf varieties have increased substantially in the state. At present there are 208 mulberry farms, 21 nurseries and 545 incubation centres.

The temporal increase in the acreage of dwarf mulberry trees is given in Table 8.6.

**Table 8.6**
**Area Under Dwarf Mulberry Trees–1984-85**

| Year | Dwarf mulberry trees Area in acres | Percentage increase |
|---|---|---|
| 1974-75 | 31 | 838.70 |
| 1978-79 | 291 | 20.27 |
| 1983-84 | 350 | – |

**Source:** Digest of Statistics. J & K Govt.

An analysis of Table 8.6 shows that in 1974-75 the dwarf variety of mulberry tree was spread in only 31 acres. Between 1975 and 1978 there had been adequate stress on dwarf varieties. Consequently, the area has increased to 291 acres in 1978-79 and 350 acres in 1983-84. The climate and skilled labour of the Valley of Kashmir put the state in an advantageous position for the spread of sericulture and silk industry. New, sturdy hybrid species of silkworm need to be developed which can with stand the adverse climatic conditions and can give withstand the adverse climatic conditions and can give increased yield and better quality of cocoons.

## Floating Gardens (Radh)

Cultivation of vegetables in and around the Dal Lake is a peculiar feature of the agricultural systems of Kashmir. The *Demb* fields and *Radh* (floating fields) are the main suppliers of vegetables to the city of Srinagar.

*Radh* (floating gardens) are made of reed in the form of strips. These strips are generally made about 2 metres wide

12. Floating Gardens and Weed Growth in Dal Lake

and 100 metres long each. Two or more than two strips are tied with ropes to make a *Radh* which may be one to two hundred metres in length. These strips can be towed from place to place and moored at the four corners by wooden poles driven into the lake bed.

When the *Radh* is made strong to bear the weight of a man, heaps of weed and mud are extracted from the lake by poles and indegenous tools. These heaps are formed into cones (*Pokar*) and placed at the *Radh* (floating field) at an interval of about two metres. Simultaneously in the month of April seeds are sown by the growers in their houses to grow seedlings. In the middle of May these seedlings of vegetables are transplanted in the Pokar (earthen and weed cone). The vegetable plants grow rapidly in the fertile and moist soil of the Pokar under the intese temperature of the period. The cool breeze provide enough moisture to the *Pokar* soil and irrigation to the crop is not required. In the floating fields, vegetables like tomatoes, cucumber, melon, and water-melon are generally grown. These crops are harvested from July to September.

**Demb-Land**

The Demb Hanj or vegetable growers have reclaimed land from the shallow waters of Dal, Nagin and Wular lakes. For the development of a *Demb*-field, a vegetable growers, selects a shallow water suitable site near the bank of the lake and plants willow poplar trees along its sides. Inside these willow and poplar trees he casts boat-loads of weed and mud until his land emerges above the level of the water and year after year he adds a new dressing of rich soil and weed obtained from the water of the lake. The two *Demb*-fields are generally separated from each other by a water-channel which helps in providing water and moisture to the crops. Through these water-channels, small boats are moved from one field to another.

The main crops grown in the *Demb*-fields are *Haak* (Spinach), pumpkins, gourd, melon, tomato, turnip, carrot, reddish, onion, chillies, letuce, egg-plant, white-beans, maize and rape-seeds.

The *Radh* and *Demb* fields are undoubtedly providing fresh vegetables to the urban population of the valley, but they are polluting the water and accelerating the rate of silting of the lakes, which may ultimately convert the beautiful lakes like Dal and Nagin into a flat fertile tract.

## Livestock

Livestock rearing is an important economic activity in the rural parts of the state. The cool climate, the alpine pastures, the perennial streams and demand for milk and milk products, all favour the keeping of cattle in Jammu and Kashmir State. Cattle, sheep, goats, horses and ponies are reared in large quantities mainly by the rural dwellers of the state. The number of cattle according to the statistics of 1983-84 were as given in Table 8.7.

**Table 8.7**
**Jammu and Kashmir State–Animal Husbandry**

| Livestock | Number in Lakh | Percentage |
|---|---|---|
| 1. Cattle | 23.25 | 3903 |
| 2. Sheep | 19.09 | 32.05 |
| 3. Goats | 10.04 | 16.86 |
| 4. Buffaloes | 5.63 | 9.45 |
| 5. Horses, ponies etc. | 1.31 | 2.20 |
| Total | 59.56 | 100.00 |

**Source:** Livestock Census, 1999-2000.

An examination of Table 8.7 shows that the total population of cattle in the state in 1982 was 59.56 lakhs, out of which 39% were cattle and 32% sheep. The percentage of goats was about 17 while buffaloes constituted 9% of the total cattle population, and horses and ponies share was only 2% in the total cattle population (Fig. 15). The dominance of cattle population is found in Udhampur, Doda, Kathua, Anantnag, Baramulla, Pulwama and Rajouri districts. Most of the stock, however, is local and inferior in quality. The

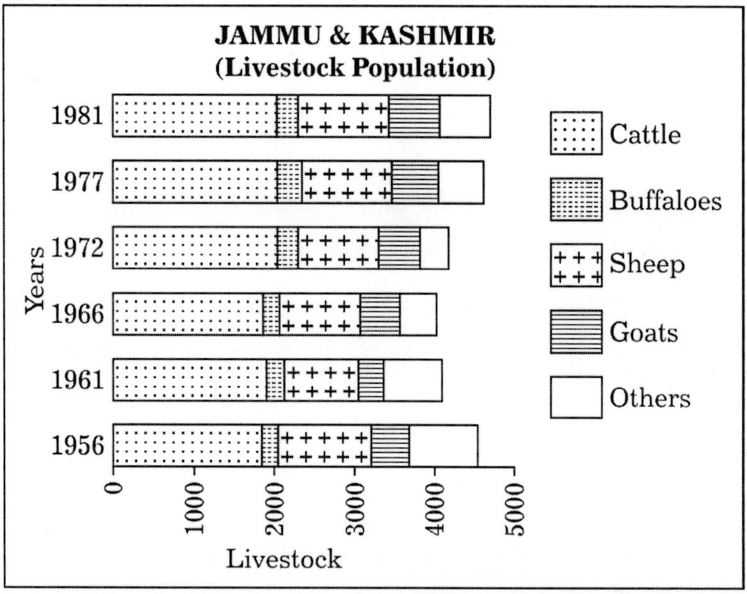


**Fig. 15 : Jammu & Kashmir–Livestock Population**

State Government is taking various step to improve the quality of cattle, sheep and goats and several such farms have been established in different parts of the state. Some of the important cattle breeding farms are:

(i) Cattle Breeding Farm Chashma-Shahi, Manasbal, Srinagar
(ii) Cattle Breeding Farm Belicharna, Jammu
(iii) Cattle Breeding Farm Changspa
(iv) Cattle cum Karakul Sheep Farm Khumbathang
(v) Yak Breeding Farm Nubra and
(vi) Veterinary Hospital Dras.

## Apiculture

Apiculture is also known as bee-keeping. In bee-keeping, bee colonies are maintained for the commercial production of honey and other bee products. Bee keeping also helps in cross pollination of crops. Honey produced by honey-bees has been considered as a balanced, delicious food for thousands of years and the honey bee is amongst the most ancient of domestic animals.

The Valley of Kashmir is well known for its great diversity of flowers ranging from lily to saffron. Most flowers are dependent upon bees for carrying pollen from the anthers (male part) of one flower to the stigmas (female part) of the flower. Many fruit trees like almond, cherry, pears, pumpkin, sunflower will not produce fruit unless bees are present to pollinate them.

In the Valley of Kashmir bee keeping is a household industry in Pampore, Srinagar, Pulwama, Tral, Kulgam, Badgam, Islamabad, Qazigund and Karnah, In Jammu Division bee keeping is being developed in Udhampur, Poonch, Kishtwar, Bhadarwah and Batote.

## Problems of Agriculture

Agriculture as discussed at the outset provides employment to over 70% of working population in the state. It also provides raw materials for a number of agro-based industries. But the agricultural sector is not developing at the desired level of development. Some of the reasons for the stunted growth of agriculture are:

(1) The average size of holdings is small. About 40% of the holdings, especially in the Jammu and Jhelum plains are less than one hectare which do not yield enough income for purchase of irrigation water, fertilizers, pesticides and new technology.

(2) In the *Kandi* areas and parts of *Karewas* irrigation is not possible owing to undulating terrain and non-availability of underground water-table. Contrary to this the poor maintenance of Zamindari Canals (*Khuls*) in the Valley of Kashmir is damaging the chemical and textural properties of the fertile soils.

(3) Soil erosion is a serious menace in the *Kandi* tracts, while unscientific rotation of crops in the plain parts are depleting the soils. In Jammu, it has been found that rice crop is followed by wheat crop in a field. Both the crops are soil exhaustive which deplete the soil fertility at a much faster rate. Moreover, the fallowing of fertile fields in Jammu is not done owing to meet the food

requirements of the people. Green manuring crops cannot be raised for the same reason. The chemical fertilizers which can help in maintenance of soil fertility are expensive and beyond the means of small cultivators efforts. Therefore need to be made to increase the use of rural compost, urban compost and sewage manures.

(4) The implements of most of the cultivators, especially in the paddy and maize growing villages of Kashmir are obsolete which were designed during the last century and inadequate to carry out agricultural operations effectively. The wooden plough and pulveriser are still most commonly used. New tools and implements should be provided to the farmers at subsidised rates.

(5) Plant protection in the entire state in general and in the High Yielding Varieties growing areas in particular should be provided for which cheap insecticides and extension service can go a long way in overcoming the problem.

(6) Agricultural marketing is another problem which the orchard and saffron growers are particularly facing. There is long distance between the apple orchards of the valley and the markets of Great Plains of India in which fruits are sold. The transportation cost makes the fruits of the valley more expansive as a result of which it is becoming increasingly difficult to compete with the apples of Himachal Pradesh and Uttranchal (Tehri, Garhwal, Kumaon).

To overcome these problems, concrete steps have to be taken. The main problems of the *Kandi* lands and plain areas have to be indentified systematically before any integrated plan for development is to be formulated.

### *References*

1. N.P.K. Aiyer, 1986, '*Field Crops of India*', Banglore.
2. M. Husain, 1979, '*Agriculture Geography*', New Delhi.
3. Govt. of India, '*Indian Agricultural*', Statistics, New Delhi.
4. *Indian Council of Agricultural Research*, Handbook of Agriculture, New Delhi, 1970
5. Govt. of J & K, 1984, *Digest of Statistics*, Srinagar.
6. G.M. Mir, '*Saffron Cultivation in Kashmir*', Srinagar.

# Chapter-IX
# Industries

The industrial development of a region largely depends on the availability of minerals, power, capital and human resources. In the location of a modern industry the importance of raw materials (minerals, forest-products, fibres, chemicals), and energy resources is so fundamental that it need no emphasising. The site of a industry is also influenced by the climatic conditions, availability of water, capital, market, skilled labour, industrial inertia, historical accident and government policy.

The State of Jammu and Kashmir, though rich in water and forest, is not fortunate in respect of basic mineral and power resources. The non-availability of iron ore, coal, petroleum and natural gas the remarkable growth of human population and the unstable geo-political conditions have put great constraints in the development of industries in the state. Nevertheless, the Kashmiris have an age old tradition in the manufacturing of carpets, silk textiles, shawls, raffle, wood-work and handicrafts. In the rural areas leather industry, village oil industry, village cereal products, pottery, blacksmithry, carpentry, bee-keeping, papier-mache, willow-wicker, soap, food-preservation and cottage match are some of the village industries which provide full or part-time employment to the people. Some of the important industries of the state have been described in the present chapter.

**Silk Textile**

The art of silk making has been practised in the state

since ancient times. Kashmiri art and craft are renowned the world over for their charm of colour and shades. Silk fabrics were exported from Kashmir to Persia (Iran), Greek and Roman Empires. During the medieval period the Mughals were the great lovers of silken cloths and they patronised this industry in the Valley of Kashmir.

At present silk industry and its allied activities provide employment to about 2.45 lakh people and contributes about four crores to the income of the state. It also helps in the building of a concrete base for the village and small scale industries (e.g. shawl, carpet, *Gabba*, *Namada*, hosiery, embroidery etc.). Moreover, it utilizes the barren and less productive tracts for the cultivation of mulberry trees. The workers engaged in the various activities of silk textile in the state are given in Table 9.1.

**Table 9.1**
**Employment in Silk Industry**

| Employment | Number | Percentage of Total workers |
|---|---|---|
| 1. Silk factories | 930 | 0.38 |
| 2. Weaving factories | 2000 | 0.81 |
| 3. Mulberry culture | 425 | 0.17 |
| 4. Staff | 700 | 0.29 |
| **Seasonal Workers** | | |
| 5. Grainage | 800 | 0.33 |
| 6. Silk worm rearing | 24,000 | 98.02 |
| Total | 2,44,755 | 100.00 |

**Source:** Govt. of J & K Digest Statistics, 1984

An examination of Table 9.1 shows that silk textile provides permanent and seasonal employment to about 2.45 lakh workers. Over 58% of the workers are, however, busy in silkworm rearing and grainage. There are only 4055 workers who work permanently in silk textile.

The silk factory at present consists of several sectors and it is dependent on various units. The basic units comprise of

(i) farmers, rearing silk-worms and production of cocoons, (ii) the second unit is the manufacturing of silk fibre and cloth. There are two silk factories in the state, situated one at Rambagh (Srinagar) and the second at Jammu, (iii) the third unit is the Department of Sericulture Development which produces improved varieties of silk worms and take care of mulberry trees.

The Rambagh Silk Factory was established in May 1897 by Raja Ranbir Singh under the guidance of Malton. The annual production data of the Rambagh Silk Factory is given in Table 9.2.

**Table 9.2**
**Silk Production–Rambagh Factory**

| Year | Production of Raw Silk in kg. |
|---|---|
| 1974-75 | 50,792 |
| 1976-77 | 44,280 |
| 1978-79 | 57,183 |
| 1980-81 | 57,850 |
| 1982-83 | 37,361 |
| 1984-85 | 42,796 |

**Source:** Data obtained from the Silk Factory Rambagh.

The Rambagh Silk Factory produces annually about 47 thousand kg. of raw silk. The silk production, however, fluctuates between 37 to 57 thousand kg. In 1980-81 for example, there was a record production of 57.85 kg. Silk which slumpped to only 37.36 kg. in 1982-83. The production of silk largely depends on the availability of mulberry leaves which constitute the main feed of silk worms.

There are various categories of workers in the Rambagh Factory performing different activities. Table 9.2 shows the number and percentage of workers who are engaged in various activities of raw silk production in Rambagh Silk Factory.

Most of the workers (82%) are busy in spinning, store-keeping and cooking while silk cleaners, knotters, waste cleaners and rewinders constitute about 81% of the total work force (Table 9.3).

**Table 9.3**
**Rambagh Silk Factory–Silk Workers-2000**

| Type of Workers | Number | Percent to the total workers |
|---|---|---|
| 1. Spinners | 322 | 34.22 |
| 2. Cooks | 170 | 18.20 |
| 3. Knotters | 35 | 3.80 |
| 4. Silk Cleaners | 54 | 5.90 |
| 5. Waste Cleaners | 51 | 5.48 |
| 6. Rewinders | 44 | 4.80 |
| 7. Store-keepers | 222 | 23.90 |
| 8. Others | 32 | 3.40 |
| Total | 890 | 100.00 |

**Source:** Silk Factory Rambagh, Srinagar.

Sericulture, despite favourable agroclimatic conditions has not grown at the desirable rate. Apart from the vigories of weather, competition from artificial silk is posing serious problems for silk industry as the artificial fibre is cheaper than the pure silk fibre. Other problems include low productivity and inferior quality of cocoons, high cost of production, absence of organised marketing agency and the stagnancy of demand.

## Carpet Making and Woollen Textile

Carpet making is an important industry of the state. Kashmiri carpets have been appreciated in and outside of the country throughout the history. Its major concentration lies in and around the city of Srinagar.

In Kashmiri carpets, the wrap is drawn in cotton, while the leave and texture leaving a fluffy pile is done by wool, silk and synthetic fibres. The number of knots in a given unit determines the quality and value of carpet together with the quality of yarn, dyestuff and the finish. Kashmiri Qaleens (carpets) are manufactured by the Government undertakings as well as by the private establishments. Some of the important carpet manufacturing centres in Srinagar are, the Cottage Industry, Exposition, C.A.E. Carpet Factory, Kashmiri Carpet Factory, G.O. Carpet Factory, The India-Kashmiri Carpet Factory, The Farghan Carpet Factory, The East India Carpet Factory, The Oriental Carpet Factory and the John Carpet Factory.

In most of these factories, children from poor families work. These workers get inadequate nutrition, and work under unhygienic conditions. Consequently, their health, efficiency and education are adversely affected. About 75% of the total carpet production is exported to the countries of Middle-East and North-West Europe (U.K., France, Holland, Denmark, Germany, Belgium), which provide exchange over one million dollars annually.

Carpet making gas many allied and ancillary crafts. *Namda* and *Gabba* are especial types of woollen carpets, used by the Kashmiris in winters. *Namda* is a type of felt made of raw wool and cotton mixed in various proportions according to its grade and quality. The average size of *Namda* is 1 metre × 1.5 metres. Srinagar city is the main centre of *Namda* manufacturing. *Gabba* is relatively large in size, being 1.75×2.50 metres in dimension. *Gabba* is made of coarse wool in black, red, yellow and green colours combinations. The *Gabbas* of Islamabad (Anantnag) are famous all over the country.

Apart from carpet making, there are two woollen textile factories one each at Karan Nagar and Bemina in the city of Srinagar. The wool textile of Nasushehra (Srinagar) produces raffle utilized mainly for shawl making. Woollen hosiery goods are produced in Jammu City. About 900 workers are engaged in the woollen textile which fetches about over Rs. 25 million annually.

## Forest Based Industries

Jammu and Kashmir State has over 30% of its total area under forest (Chapter 3). Most of the forests consist of conifers which provide soft, valuable wood. These forests, if utilized properly can sustain a number of industries. Paper,

13. Kashmiri baker

pulp, match, sports goods, furniture, joinery, toys making are a few industries which can be developed in the *Kandi* and rural areas of the state.

Although a number ofjoinery mills have been established in Srinagar, especially along the Srinagar-Baramulla Road, Pampore. Jammu, and sports goods are being manufactured at Miransahib (Jammu) and in the villages of Anantnag District, yet planned efforts have to be made to develop forest based industries in the state. The willow mulberry and walnut trees can provide the raw-materials required for the development of sports goods, furniture and wood artificials. About two thousand workers earn their livelihood from forest based industries and their annual production is worth Rs. 25 million.

Forests also provide turpentine and a variety of resins, used in many industries. Resin is collected from the pine trees of Jammu and Kashmir Divisions. It has diversified properties. Lac obtained from the forests can be utilized in the manufacturing of polish, gramophone-records, adhesives, printing ink etc. There are resin manufacturing centers at Miransahib, Sunderbani and Rajouri. These three factories employ 325 workers and produce resin worth Rs. 5 lakhs.

## Agro-based Industries

The State of Jammu and Kashmir is primarily agricultural. In fact, agricultural products not only yield over 55% of the state income but also provides raw materials to a number of industries. Fruit-canning, edible-oils factories, derive raw materials from agriculture.

The Jammu Division and Kashmir-Valley produce large quantities of paddy. Over 60% of the total population of the state is rice eater. The husk of paddy is removed in rice mills before it is marketed as rice. There are several large and small sized rice mills in the state. Babarshah (Srinagar) has a large rice mill, but a modern rice plant was established at Laithpore in 1981 (near Pampore). The rice husk and rice bran are used as fuel and animal feed respectively. Bran is also used for the extraction of fatty-oil which finds application in soap industry.

The Valley of Kashmir has large tracts under apple, almonds, walnut, cherry, peach and pear orchards. Transportation of these perishable fruits to the distant markets by road is quite expensive. The processing of fruits and making of jam, jelley, juice etc. are some of the industries which have enormous potential especially in the districts of Baramulla and Anantnag. The Food Corporation of India (FCI) has to take initiative in this direction. Some fruit-based industries are however, coming up in the Valley of Kashmir.

**Cement Industry**

The raw materials for the manufacturing of cement are calcareous and argillaceous materials. These are mixed in suitable proportions to from the raw mix limestone, gypsum, coal, bauxite and clay are the main ingredients of this industry. Limestone and gypsum are available in large quantities in the Baramulla and Anantnag Districts.

The Wuyan Cement Factory was established in 1962 in which the raw materials obtained from Uri and Baramulla are used. This factory provides employment to about 200 workers and produces annually about 200 tonnes of cement per day. Recently (1982) a large cement factory has been set up at Khrew, known as the J & K Cements Ltd. Khrew. There are 500 workers employed in this factory producing about 600 tonnes of cement a day.

There are several chemicals manufacturing units, tile-factory (Pampore), lignite briquetting plant (Shalateng, glass making and electric goods manufacturing units in the state.

In the Public Sector, a Hindustan Machine Tools (H.M.T.) Watch Factory has been established at Zainakot. It provides employment to about 1300 workers and produces about 4.50 lakhs watches annually, equivalent to Rs. 120 millions.

At Hyderpora (Srinagar), the Indian Telephone Industry has been established. It is a branch of the Indian Telephone Industry, Banglore which produces telephone parts and accessories. It is a small unit in which only 150 workers find employment and telephone parts worth Rs. 20 million are produced annually.

## Industrial Complexes

The State Government in recent years has been paying attention towards the development of light and agro-based industries. The State Industrial Development Corporation has established industrial complexes at Rangreth, Khunamoh and Doabgah in Kashmir and at Bari-Brahmanan in Jammu.

The Rangreth Factory assembles television sets, radios, transistors, electronic clocks, stabilizers, electric blankets, tape recorders and jewels for watches. Joinery articles, matches, automobile batteries and tiles are manufactured at Khonamoh. Bari-Brahmanan has become an important industrial complex of Jammu, producing detergents, resin-products, vanaspati, steel-rolling, scooters, textiles, sunmica, paper, pistons, hosiery, electric-goods, light machines, rubber and plastic goods, chemicals, drugs, paper, printing, transport goods etc.

There are assorted village industries in the state. Leather processing, shoe making, oil pressing, pottery, black-smithry, carpentry, bee-keeping, basket making, soap making, fruit preservation etc. are the main industries in which the rural population is finding employment.

The State of Jammu and Kashmir which has not seen much of industrial growth due to lack of basic minerals and infrastructures has started showing the signs of industrialization. The development of new power projects, wide-spread of roads-network and coming up of the state on the railway map of the country have helped appreciably in creating an atmosphere conducive for the growth and development of industries. A number of industrial areas have been set up and various steps are being taken to help the development of industries. The number of registered factories has gone upto 670 and about 1500 are small scale industries. Concerted efforts need to be made in this direction, failure to which the industrial sector of the state may show stunted growth.

## Chapter-X

# Tourism

Tourism at present is the largest industry in the world. Tourism frames massive and continuous flow of people to more and more all around the globe. In recent years, tourism has undergone several major shifts. Now tourism is an organised industry in which have entered the multinationals. The means of transport which can carry people in bulk to far-off places has increased rapidly and the increase in the size of range of jet aircraft has led to the creation of a long-haul package holiday market, for example Thailand, that hardly existed a decade ago. The objectives of tourists also varies in space and time. This emerging pattern of tourism is transforming the socio-economic patterns and cultural values of the people all over the world.

The practice of holiday-making away from one's normal place of residence to known as tourism. Tourists are defined as people visiting a place other that in which they normally reside, for a period including as overnight stay, for any reason other than following an occupation remunerated in the place visited. This operational definition, therefore, includes certain people travelling for reasons other than holiday-making (e.g., conference participants, pilgrims) but it is normally impracticable to exclude them when data are collected. The distinction between *recreation* and *tourism* is that recreation involves leisure activities of *less* than 24 hour's duration away from home, whereas tourism involves a longer time scale and therefore, requires more infrastructure in the form of accommodation provision.[1] The International Association of

Scientific Experts on Tourism (AIEST) has defined tourism as the sum of phenomena and relationship arising from the travel and stay of nonresidents, in so far as they do not lead to permanent residence and are not connected with any earning activity.

The essence of the tourist economy is that the tourist spends, in the chosen holiday area, money that has been earned elsewhere. Charistaller (1964) has pointed out that tourism is a very important free-market agent of the spatial redistribution of wealth.[2] In any economy, tourism acts as an export sector, bringing money into the area, setting up both income multipliers creating jobs.

The history of tourism is as old as the human society itself. The early tourism can be traced from the period when man set sail and attempted to know the immediate world around. His inherent zeal for enchanted unknown lands and curiosity for new world culminated into early travels. At the start of the present century, travel and tourism were confined only to affluent few, i.e. rich, religious zealots, conquerors, the well educated and the elites who were fascinated by the enchanting beauty and mysteries of unknown land.[3] Tourism has, however, grown from the pursuits of a privileged few to a mass movement of people, with the urge to discover the unknown places and to seek change in environment and to undergo new experiences.[4]

The dramatic transformation of rudimentary tourism into a giant phenomenon has resulted from a set of physico, socio-economic, political, psychological and aesthetic factors. Modern tourism upsurged after the Second World War commencing with a spurt in human mobility and intensive application of mechanizations.[5] In the ending part of the $18^{th}$ century, industrialization resulted into commercialism and urbanization. Consequently, the standard of living of the people went up and there was a concomitant rise in leisure hours compelling people to adopt travel and recreation as an inevitable lifestyle. Also, within a short span, human members increased tremendously particularly in the urban centres.

All these factors culminated into ushering a new wave of migration, typically termed as 'Mass Tourism'. At present, touring and outdoor recreation have become a genuine social, economic and psychological need, not for individuals alone but also for our entire society and economy. Tourism development holds immense appeal because of anticipated economic benefits of income and employment.[6] In terms of employment, it is the largest industry that provides jobs to about one in every 16 workers worldwide.[7] It helps in removing the regional disparities, particularly in under developed and backward areas.[8]

Kashmir is one of the most beautiful tourist destinations in the world. It used to attract enormous number of domestic and international tourists before 1989. The period between 1989 and 2004 is a lean period from the tourists point of view. The unstable political situation of the state, the militancy and slogan of *Azadi* (independence) discouraged the tourists and recreation-seekers.[9] Tourism, however, is a dominant economic activity in the state as about 20% of the workforce of the state is directly or indirectly dependent on tourism.

After agriculture, tourism is the main economic activity in the state. The Jammu and Kashmir state is quite rich in renewable resources (water, forest and fresh air) and scenic beauty. Its lush green forests, rich wildlife, snow-clad peaks, mountainous gorges, giant glaciers, rich fishing grounds, lofty skiing grounds, carpet green turfs, perennial rivers, gushing fountains, floating gardens in Dal Lake, hissing springs, cool breeze, shimmering lakes, invigorating climate, apple-almond, orchard, saffron fields and benevolent and kind hearted folk are well known all over the world. In the absence of basic mineral (iron-ore, copper, coal, petroleum etc.) its productive fields, valuable forests, water and invigorating climate are the great bounties of nature.

## Tourism in Kashmir Division

As stated at the outset, Kashmir is one of the most beautiful regions of the world. Characterized with young folded mountains, deep gorges, waterfalls, cascades, scenic beauty and alpine pastures, the state of Jammu and Kashmir provides great opportunities for the domestic and international tourists. In the following paragraphs a brief description of the major places of tourists-interest and the games and outdoor activities the tourists can perform, have been given.

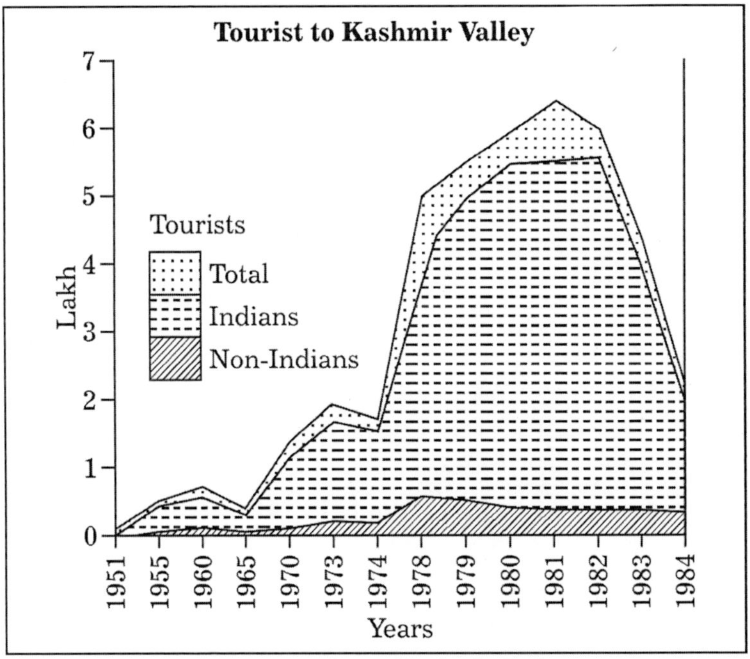


**Fig. 16 : Tourist to Kashmir Valley**

## Around Srinagar

Srinagar, the summer capital of the state of Jammu and Kashmir is situated around the Dal Lake and on both the sides of the Jhelum River. It has many places of interest for the national and international tourists. Having a population of about 7 lakh, it is the primate city in the Valley of Kashmir. It has most of the cultural, educational, religious, recreational and business centres. Apart from the Dal and Nagin lakes the tourists are attracted by the shrines of Hazrathal, Shah Hamdan Mosque, Ziarat (tomb) of Zain-ul-Abidin, Jama

14. Tourist Enjoying Water-skiing in Dal Lake.

15. Indian Tourists at Chashma Shahi

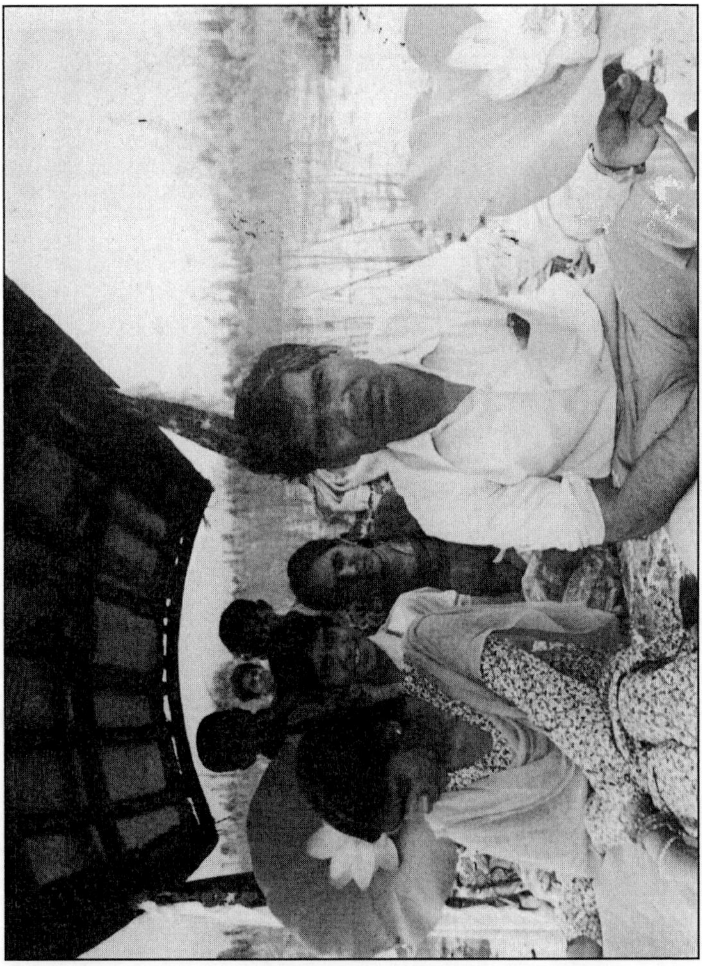

16. Tourists Shikara-Ride

Masjid, Shankaracharya (Takht-e-Sulaiman). Hari-Parbat Fort, Panderthan Temple, Harwan, the Pratap Singh Museum, Mughal Gardens–Shalimar, Nishat, Chashmashahi, Naseem Bagh and Dachigam National Park.

## Dal Lake

The Dal Lake and its houseboats are one of the main attractions for tourists in Kashmir. The Mughals developed exquisite and elegant gardens like Nishat, Shalimar, Chashma Shahi, Pari Mahal and Naseem Bagh on or around its bank. Some of the Mughal Gardens are excellently maintained even to this day. During the Raj period, Kashmiri rulers did not permit the British (who were as fond of Kashmiri's cool climate as the Mughals) to own land here. So they adopted the superbly British solution of building houseboats a float on Dal Lake. A visit to Kashmir, it is often said is not complete until you have stayed in a houseboat. Subsequently, the Nehru Park and Dal Patti near Hazratbal were developed as the places of attraction for the tourists.

The lake has been divided into three parts (i) Gagribal, (ii) Lokut-dal and (iii) Bod-dal. Dal Gate, at the city end of the lake, controls the flow of the lake water into the Jhelum River. Within the lake are two islands which are popular picnic spots, i.e., Sona Lanka (Gold Island) and Rupa Lanka (Silver Island). Both are also known as Char-Chinar, because each one of them has four chinar trees. There is third Island, Nehru Park, at the end of the, main stretch of the lake side Boulevard. The water of the lake is however, highly polluted these days. There is no sewage disposal system and all the waste from the houseboats goes straight into the lake. The floating fields in the lake and the sediments deposited by the Telbal Nala are the outer pollutants of the lake. The process of eutripication has accentuated by the application of chemical fertilizers in the paddy fields of the Dachigam-Telbal Nalla, catchment.

Despite all these ecological problems, the Dal Lake is a great attraction for the tourists. In fact, the water dwellers

(Hanjis) have a distinct way of life who stay in the water throughout their lives and are buried on the mainland (graveyards) after their deaths. One may observe the mobile shops of vegetables, grocery, mutton, cloths, cosmetics and chemists in the Dal Lake. Thus, a shikara circuit of the lake is a sybaritic experience not to be missed. A leisurely cruise around will takeone day, including visit to the Mughal Gardens.

The Boulevard, running along side Dal Lake, is quite attractive for the tourists. The Shikara Ghats provide access to the houseboats, hotels, restaurant and shops along the way. Other main roads of the city are the Residency Road, connecting the Tourist Reception Centre with the down town area and the Polo View Road lined with handicraft shops and travel agencies.

Kashmiris are gifted handicraft-makers and have great dexterity in artificants. The popular products which attract the tourists are carpets, papier-mache articles, leather and fur goods, wood carving, shawls, scarves, embroidery, honey, cardigans, knitted sweaters and walnut wood articles, Saffron, honey, apples, almond, walnut and dry apricot are also much in demand in the tourist industry.[10]

## Gulmarg

Gulmarg, literally means '*the meadow of flower*'. It is considered as one of the unparalleled hill resorts in the world. Gulmarg is a wide, green, undulating valley characterized by eskers and terminal moraines, and surrounded by dense fir forests. Situated in the lap of the Pir Panjal Range it is a unique place intersected by the fresh-water channels, dotted over with wood villages. Looking downwards towards the Firozpur Nallah is the vast levelled land devoted to paddy crop in summer season. On a clear day, Nanga Parbat is visible to the north and Harmukh and Sunset Peak are visible to the south-east.

There are numerous buses running from Srinagar to Gulmarg, many of them of the day tours. The Tourists Hotel,

17. Tourist Playing Golf in Gulmarg, Kashmir

City View Hotel, Tourist Bungalow, the Highway Hotel, Kingsley Hotel, the Green View and Gulmarg Hotel are the reasonable places to stay. Ahdoo's Hotel, next to the bus stand is probably the best place to eat at Gulmarg. A circular road, 11 km. in length, runs right round Gulmarg through pleasant pine forest with excellent views over Kashmir Valley.[11]

About a six kilometre walk from the Gulmarg bus stop is the important meadow of Khilanmarg. The meadow carpeted with flowers in the spring, is the site for Gulmarg's winter skiing runs and offers a fine view of the surrounding peaks and the Kashmir Valley. During the early springs (mid-March to April) as the snow metls, it can be a very muddy hour's climb upto the Khilanmarg meadow.

Gulmarg is famous for winter sports, especially skiing. There is one chair lift, one T-bar and four pomas. All lift operate from 10 a.m. to 5 p.m. A new cable car has been constructed to the top of Mt. Apharwat, Ridge, and this has opened up some superb new areas above the tree line.

About 13 km from Gulmarg, beyond Khilanmarg at the foot of Apharwat Peak (4511 m) is the location of Alpather Lake. This lake remains frozen until mid-June, and even later in the year one can see lumps of ice-floating in its cold waters. The walk from Gulmarg follows a well-graded pony track over the 3,810 m Apharwat Ridge, separating the lake from Khilanmarg.

In addition to these points and places of attraction, there is *Ziarat* of Baba Rishi. This famous Muslim shrine is on the slopes below Gulmarg and can be reached from either Gulmarg or Tanmarg. The *Ziarat* or tomb, is of a well-known Muslim who died here in 1480 A.D. Before renouncing worldly ways he was a courtier of the Kashmir King Zain-ul-Abidin.[12]

Gulmarg is the premier skiing resort. The Ski-club of India was established in Gulmarg provide runs ranging from below 200 m to 2,000 m and an altitude difference of over 1,500 m, with length of more than 10 km. Moreover, numerous ski-slopes, graded for various levels of skiers, there is a chair-

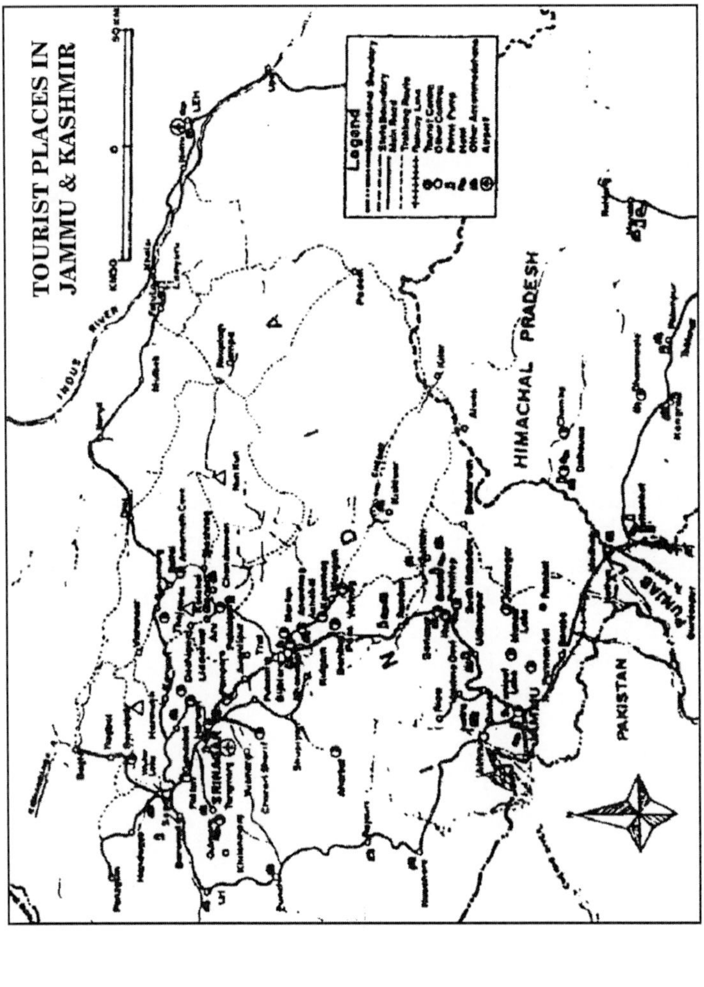


Fig. 17 : Tourist Places in Jammu & Kashmir

lift of a length of 500 m, providing a ski-run of 700 m. Among the multitude of slopes, there are a few which are served by ski-lift. Most of the skiing becomes centred around these slopes, which are especially suited to beginners and intermediate level skiers. With the construction of "Poma Ski-Gopndola Cable Cat", designed by Polamgalski of France, Gulmarg to Apherwat, the destination offers ski-run for every level including for the most advanced and the most Adventurists.

Gulmarg has the distinction of being Asia's only Heli-skiing Resort Heli-skiing was introduced by Sylvan Saudan in Gulmarg in 1987. In this sport, a helicopter takes the skier up to the Apherwat Peak from where they choose their own descent route. One can mark new tracks almost throughout the entire winter season. There are long chains of mountain valleys and ridges covered with fine powder snow. One can even try a different valley each day with the aid of a helicopter.

**Pahalgam**

Pahalgam situated at the bank of Lidder River is considered as one of most beautiful tourist sites in the world. It is about 95 km from Srinagar and at 2,130 m above the sea level. The beautiful Lidder River flows right through the town, which is at junction of the Sheshnag and Lidder rivers and is surrounded by soaring, fir and deodar covered mountains with snow-capped peaks rising behind them.

There are many short walks from Pahalgam and it is an ideal base for longer treks to Kolahoi Glacier or Amarnath Cave. Pahalgam is also famous for many of its shepherds. There are common sight, driving their flocks of sheep along the *paths* all around the town.

In the vicinity of Pahalgam are the places of tourists interests like Mamaleswara, Baisaran, Aru and Chandanwari, Mamaleswara is only one km downstream and on the right bank of the Lidder. There is a small Shiva Temple at Mamaleswara, Baisaran is a meadow. There are excellent views over the town and the Lidder Valley from this meadow, five km from Pahalgam. A further 11 km is situated the Tulian Lake at a height of 3,353 m above the sea-level. It is covered with ice for most of the year. Aru is a small village at a distance of about 11 km upstream. It is situated at the Pahalgam-Kolahoi Glacier trek (Fig. 18). Just outside of Pahalgam on the Amarnath route the *Yog Niketan Ashram* is an interesting place to stay and take *Yoga* and meditation course.

Pahalgam, initially a shepherd's village is one of the world's famous resorts and is well known for pony riding, camping sites, trout fish and rarefied clean atmosphere.

## Sonmarg

Situated in the Sindh Valley along the Srinagar-Leh, Sonmarg is an excellent base for trekking. Sonmarg means '*meadow of gold*' which could derive from the spring flowers or from the strategic position it once enjoyed. Sonmarg is situated at the terminal moraines of Thajwas Glacier. Altitudinally, it is 2,740 m above the sea level at a distance of 83 km from Srinagar (Fig. 18). The tiny village of Baltal is the last settlement in Kashmir, right at the foot of the Zoji La. The Zoji La is the watershed between Kashmir and Ladakh. Thus, Sonmarg area is sheer scenic splendour. The Sindh Valley is surrounded by mountains scaling 9,300 m in height.[13]

Sonmarg has a string of shimmering waterfalls and Thajwas Glacier. Gadsar and Satsar lakes are on the periphery of Sonmarg. The Sindh River meanders across the valley and abounds in trouts and Mahaseer-an angler's delight. The other recreational activities here include horse-riding, mountaineering, trekking and fishing. There are tourist huts, a rest house, and some small hotels, restaurants and handicrafts shopping complex.

## Kokernag

Situated at an altitude of 2,020 m, Kokernag is at a distance of about 70 km from the Tourists Reception Centre (TRC) Srinagar. It is famous for the curative properties of springs.

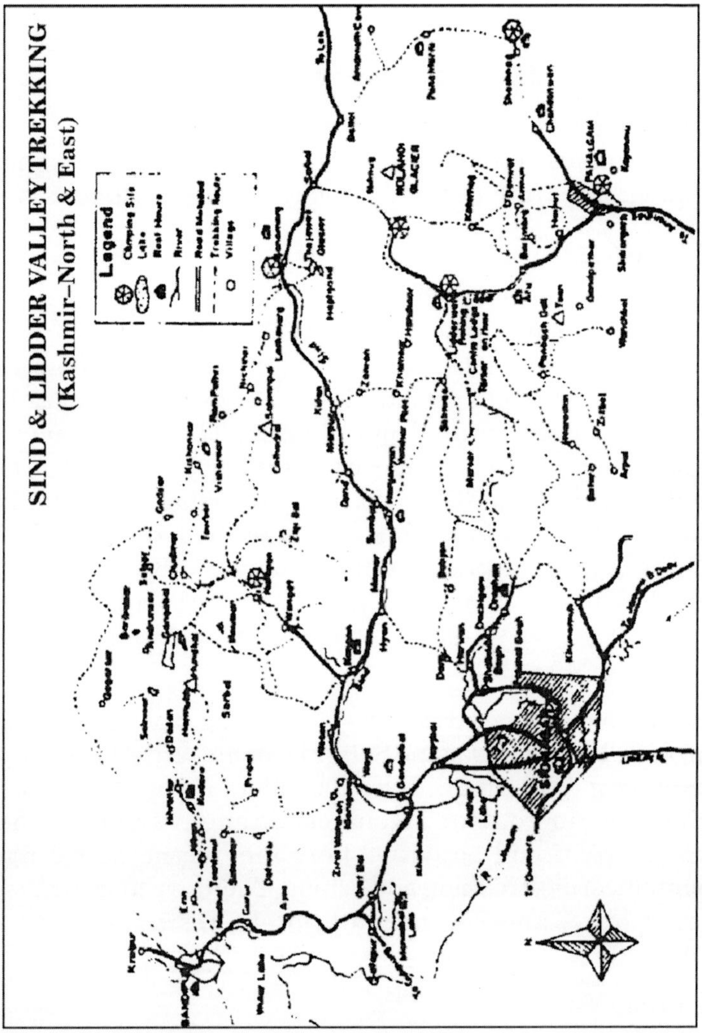


Fig. 18 : Sind & Lidder Valley Treking ( Kashmir – North & East)

It also has a botanical garden with a variety of roses. The Department of Fisheries has collaborated with a Danish firm for large-scale trout breeding at Kokernag. This useful project will annually result in the introduction of fish into the streams. At present, it is being used for the supply of table fish. Kokernag has a Tourist Bungalow, Tourist Huts and a Cafeteria run by the State Tourism Department.

### Aharbal

Situated at an altitude of 2,400 m at the debaunching point of the Vishav River, Aharbal waterfall (25m) attracts a large number of picnic goes during the summer and autumn seasons. It is about 51 km from Srinagar. It has Tourist Bungalow run by the State Tourism Department and a Rest House of the Public Work Department. A charming woodland meadow at Kungwattan is about 5 km ahead. Further ahead at a distance of about 11 km lies the Kousernag Lake which generally remains frozen and covered with icebergs till late June.

### Achabal

Situated in the District of Anantnag, Achabal is famous for the Mughal Gardens, which was developed at the spot where a smaller river comes out gushing out from the limestone topography of the mountain side. Achabal is surrounded with villages alive with running water and completely over shadowed by massive chinar trees. The garden has a straight line of fountains and waterfalls and an avenue of chinar on one side. At the head of this beautiful garden is the mountains slope covered with deodar forest. It is majestic and remarkable sight.

Achabal is about 58 km away from the Srinagar Tourist Reception Centre, situated at an altitude of about 1,667m. Once the pleasure retreat of Empress Noor Jahan, it has a fine garden, water cascades, cataracts, fine camping ground and a trout hatchery. The Maharaja of Kashmir once pitched a pretty camp here for the entertainment of Lord Minto. Lodging facilities are available in the State Tourism

Department, Tourist Bungalow and Tourist Huts.

**Yusmarg**

Yusmarg situated at an altitude of about 2,377 m is about 40 km from the Tourist Reception Centre, Srinagar (Fig. 18). It is a small open vale in the Pir Panjal Range. Giant pines, fires, spruce and deodar cover the mountain slopes on either side of the valley. Pony-riding is the other recreational activity of this silent and tranquil *Marg*. The Nil-Nag Lake can be visited from Yusmarg. Boarding and lodging facilities are available in the State Tourism Department Bungalow and the Rest House. There are several Tourist Huts to accommodate the tourists.

**Daksum**

Situated in the district of Anantnag, it is an enchanting resort griddled by mountains (Fig. 18). It is about 2,438 m above the sea level at a distance of about 85 km from Srinagar. This resort is more peaceful and less spoilt. From Daksum one can cross to Kishtwar Town of the Doda District (Jammu Division) through the Sinthan Pass.

The places of cultural tourism in Kashmir include Takht-e-Sulaiman (Shankaracharya), in Srinagar, Hari-Parbat Fort, (Srinagar), Pari Mahal, Harwan (once the abode of a famous Buddhist saint), Pandrathan (original city of Srinagar), Awantipora (after Raja Awantivarman who ruled Kashmir from 854 to 883 AD), Martand (this temple is known as the House of Pandus), Verinag (one of the sources of Jhelum), Prihaspora (built by Lahitaditya), and Pattan.

The lakes, rivers and streams of Kashmir also provide enormous opportunities for water-skiing, white water rafting, canoeing, cruising, ankling, fishing, golfing, cycling, pony-riding, hang-gliding (hot air ballooning) and trekking.

**Treks in Kashmir**

Being surrounded by the Pir Panjal and the Greater Himalayas, Kashmir provides enormous opportunities for the tourists. There are various treks both within Kashmir and form Kashmir to Ladakh, Zanskar, Kishtwar, Bhaderwah, Rajouri and Poonch. The short Pahalgam to Kolahoi Glacier Trek is particularly most popular and the Pahalgam to Amarnath Cave Trek is well known, not only for the natural scenery, but for the great religious festival that takes place annually in the month of the July.[14]

## Pahalgam to Kolahoi Glacier

This short and very popular trek takes only four days from Pahalgam to Pahalgam (Fig. 18). The first day from Pahalgam takes you to Aru along the bank of Lidder River. The second day's walk takes you to Lidderwat which has a government rest house and a very pleasant campsite, and where the stream from the glacier meets the stream from Tarsar Lake. On the third day trekup to the lake and back to Lidderwat. The glacier climbing from 3,400m to 4,000m, descend from the 5,485m Kolahoi Mountain. On their fourth day you can either walk straight back to Pahalgam in one day or the trek can be extended another day by walking from Lidderwat to Tarsar Lake and back.

Instead of returning to Pahalgam, three days further trek will take you to Kulan, near Sonmarg in the Sindh Valley (a tributary of Jhelum). It is only 16 km from Kulan to Sonmarg which you can walk or travel by bus.

## Pahalgam to Amarnath Cave

Amarnath is a sacred religious place of Hindus. The pilgrimage to Amarnath is performed annually in the month of July. At the full noon in the month of July-August, thousands of Hindu pilgrims make the *Yatra* to the Shri Amarnath Cave when a natural ice-lingam (stalactite), the symbol of Lord Shiva, reaches its greatest size.

The first days walk out of Pahalgam can be done by jeep and from Amarnath it is possible to continue north to Baltal near Sonmarg, although that is a difficult trek.

### Sonmarg to Wangat

This 81 km trek takes five days and reaches a maximum altitude of 4,191 m. It starts from Sonmarg (reached by bus from Srinagar), then climbs to Nichinai, crosses a mountain chain and drops down to the pleasant campsite at Kishansar. Another pass has to be crossed on days 3 and 4 when you reach Gangabal Lake. From here it is a steep descent to Wangat, from where you easily bus back to Srinagar.

### Gangabal Trek

This is 61 km trek which also goes to Gangabal but from the other side. The trek commences from Erin, north of Wular Lake, and takes five days in all. On the fourth day you need rope and ice-access to cross the glacier between the Kundsar and Gangabal lakes. The final day's trek also ends at Wangat. At Naranag, just before Wangat, there is an interesting old temple.

### Kausarnag Trek

This is a short trek in the south of the Kashmir Valley which ascends into the Pir Panjal mountain. The first day's trek is a short walk, only taking about three hours. With an early start from Srinagar you can bus Aharbal he and complete the first walk in the same day. Kausarnag Lake is a beautiful deep-blue stretch of water at 3,700m.

### Daksum to Kishtwar

Starting from the south Kashmir Valley at Daksum, this trek is an interesting route to Jammu, although you can also trek from Kishtwar into the *Zanskar* Valley or to Himachal Pradesh. Daksum is about 100 km from Srinagar and takes about three hours by road. The maximum altitude is reached on the first day's trek to Sinthan Pass. On the last day it is only a short Dadhpath from where buses depart at 10 am. and 4 pm. to Kishtwar.

### Pahalgam to Panikhar

This is a hard trek into the Suru Valley which leads to

Zanskar. The first two days of the trek follow the Amarnath Cave route. The following days cross the Gulol Gali Pass, climb to the Lonvilad Gali, go over the Chalong Glacier and continue down to Pannikhar. From Panikhar. From Panikhar you can take the road north to Kargil or east into the Zanskar Valley.

## Tourism in Jammu

The Jammu Division of Jammu and Kashmir State is essentially hilly excepting the southern plain along the border of Punjab. The undulating and mountainous topography is drained by the Chenab and Ravi rivers and their tributaries. The incised meanders, gorges, cataracts, river terraces and the snow covered peaks and pine and oak covered slopes present enchanting sights for the tourists. The tourism potential of the state has however, not been adequately developed in the region. It is the cultural tourism in Jammu region which is attracting more tourists and generating more income for the state.

Jammu with a population of over three lakhs is the summer capital and the second largest town of the state. For most of the tourists, who visit Kashmir, It is the transit point. There are however, several interesting points in the city which fascinate the tourists. Some of the historical and cultural centres which may be visited in Jammu city are as under.

### Raghunath Temple

The Raghunath Temple is the centre of the city, only a short stroll from tourist reception centre. This large temple complex was built in 1835. The Rambireswar Temple, also centrally located, is dedicated to Lord Shiva and dates from 1883.

### Amar Mahal Palace

On the northern outskirts of the town, just off the Srinagar Road, is the Amar Mahal Palace, a curious example of French architecture. The palace museum has a family portrait gallery and another important collections of paintings.

## Dogra Art Gallery

The Dogra Art Gallery in the Gandhi Bhavan near the secretariat has an important collection of miniature paintings, including many from the locally renowned Basholi and Kangra School. The gallery remains open from 7:30 a.m. to 1 pm. in summer and from 11 a.m. to 5 p.m. in winter but is closed on Monday.

## Vaishno Devi

Vaishno Devi is an important pilgrimage centre for the Hindus. It is situated in the Lesser Himalayas near Katra. This temple situated in a limestone cave is dedicated to the three mother goddesses of Hinduism. About fifteen lakh (1.5 million) pilgrims visit the Vaishno Devi each year after making a 12 km steep climb from a new road. The annual turn out of the *Vaishno Devi Trust* is about 2,000 crores. The Trust is so rich that often the State Government of Jammu and Kashmir, borrow money from the Vaishno Devi Trust to pay the salaries of its employees.

### *Patnitop*

Patnitop having an altitude of 2,024 m above the sea level is an important hill resort between Kud in the south and Batote in the north. Patnitop is intended to be the nucleuse of tourist development in this area, and there are tourist huts, a rest house and a youth hostel.

### *Kud*

Kud is a small township about 6 km south of Patnitop. This is a popular lunch stop on the Jammu to Srinagar route at 1,738 m above the sea level. There is well-known mountain spring, Swami ki Bauli about 1.5 km from the road.

### *Batote*

Only 12 km further on, and connected to Patnitop and Kud by number of footpaths, this hill resort at 1,560 m was the overnight stop between Jammu and Srinagar before the Banihal Tunnel was opened. As in Kud, there is a spring close to the town of Batote, known as Amrit Chasma. This spring is about 2.5 km away from Batote. There is a tourist Bungalow, tourist huts and several private hotels in Batote.

### *Sudh Mahadev*

Sudh Mahadev is situated about 8 km to the east of Kud or Panitop. There is a Shiva Temple at Sudh Mahadev which is visited by a large number of pilgrims on Asadh Purnima (full moon in July-August). About 5 km from Sudh Mahadev is Man Talai, where some archaeological discoveries have been made.

### *Sunisar and Mansar Lakes*

East of Jammu, these lakes are picturesque and the scene of an annual festival at Mansar.

### *Kishtwar*

Well known for the mining of precious stones (agate, ruby, etc.) Kishtwar is situated in the Doda district of the Jammu Division. It is connected with Jammu City by a metalled road. There is a trekking route from Kishtwar to Srinagar via Sinthan Pass. There are many waterfalls around Kishtwar, and about 19 km from the town is the pilgrimage site of Sarthal Devi.

### *Bhadarwah*

It is also known as mini Kashmir. This beautiful valley attracts a large number of tourists every year. Every two years a procession of pilgrims walk from this beautiful high altitude valley to 4,400 m high Kaplash Lake. A week later the three day Mela Patt festival takes place in Bhadarwah. There is a Rest House in this scenic location.

### *Jawahar Tunnel*

This tunnel also known as Banihal Tunnel joins Jammu with Srinagar. During the winter season (December to March) the Valley of Kashmir was often completely cut off from the rest of India before this tunnel was completed in

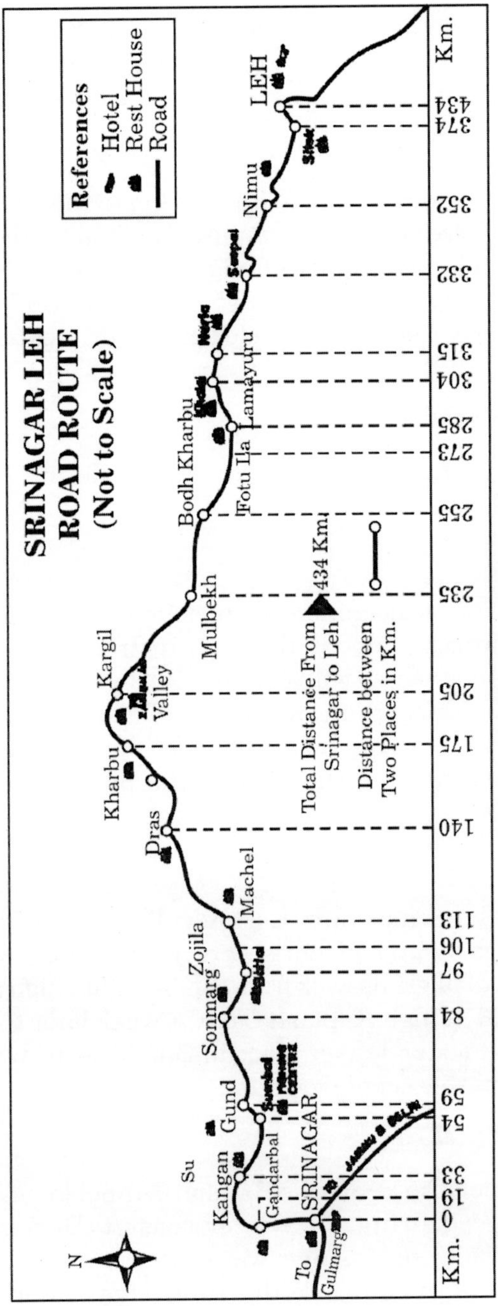


Fig. 19 : Srinagar Leh–Road Route

1967. The 2,225 m long tunnel is 200 km from Jammu and 93 km from Srinagar and has two separate passages. It is rough and damp inside as the water seepages from the roof of the tunnel. As soon as you emerge from the tunnel you are in the lush green, Vale of Kashmir.

## Tourism in Ladakh

Ladakh is also known as '*Little Tibet*', '*the Moonland*' and '*the last Shangir La*'. Ladakh is a high altitude plateau to the north of the Himalayas. It is a miniature version of *Tibet*, the people are Tibetan in their culture and religion, and there are many Tibetan refugees in Ladakh.

The Himalayas are a very effective barrier to rain-few clouds creep across their awesome height and as a result Ladakh is a barren cold desert in which the rate of evaporation is higher than the rate of precipitation. Wherever, irrigation water is available, the land is highly productive. Plant life is confined to the places where glaciers or melting snow carry water to habitation and alluvial cones. Since Ladakh is barren and dry like the rocks of the moon, it called as the '*Moonland*'.

Ladakh could well be a last Shangir La as only in mid-1970s, it was opened to *outside* visitors. Its strategic isolation is matched by its physical isolation, only from June to September is the road into Ladakh from Kashmir not covered by snow and only since 1979 has there been airline flights into Ladakh. That flight is one of the most spectacular in the world.

Ladakh is a strage worldly place-strange gompas perched on soaring hilltops, shattered-looking landscapes spalshed with small but brilliant patches of green and ancient palaces climbing to sheer rock walls. But most of all, there are the delightful Ladakhis, *friendly* as only Tibetan people can be and immensely colourful. Ladakh, the highest region in India, comprising deep and narrow valleys between the gigantic mountain ranges of the Himalayas and the Karakoram is one of the India's largest districts. The average height ranges between 3,000 m and 3,650 m above the mean sea level.

Ladakh's climate is one of sharp contrasts, but it is in this fact itself that its beauty lies. Thousand of feet high, with desolate rocks below and the blue canopy of the sky above, Ladakh has an elusive attraction. A climatic wasteland, it is an aesthetic paradise. For those with a spirit of adventure and enterprise, for those with a love for virgin nature and for those with interest in Tibetology and Buddhism, Ladakh offers an experience that is both rare and transforming.[15]

Ladakh *comprises* of two district, namely, Leh and Kargil, in the state of Jammu and Kashmir. It is connected with the Kashmir Valley by the Srinagar Leh Road (Fig. 3). This road winds its way past the Dras Valley Kargil, Ladakh's second largest town with a population of about 40,000, mainly Muslims of the Shia sect.

To the south-east of Kargil lies the largest town of Ladakh-Leh. In the past, Leh was the commercial centre of Central Asia, where numerous languages were spoken and all sorts of goods were traded. Leh, about 3,505 m above the sea level, is a small town of about 1,00,000 people. From here Leh-Manali Road proceeds to Himachal Pradesh.

Srinagar to Leh is about 434 km by road which follows the Indus River for most of the distance. Buses ply along this road daily during the summer season and take two days with two overnight stops at Kargil. Sonmarg is the major town in Kashmir, shortly before you climb up over the Zoji La Pass (3,529 m) and enter the Dras Valley of the Ladakh Division (Fig. 3).

**Zoji La**

This is one of the few unsurfaced stretches on the route. It is also the first pass to snow in winter and the last to be cleared in summer. It is not, however, the highest pass along the route. The other passes get less snow because they are across the Himalayas and in the mountain rainshadow. The road up the pass is breath-taking and there are times when you will wonder if you were sane to make this trip.

### Dras

This is the first village after the Zoji La Pass and the place from where road crews clear the road upto the pass for the start of the summer season. In winter, Dras records upto 45°C and is one of the coldest palces of India.[16]

### Kargil

One of the important trading centres, Kargil is the district headquarters on the way to Leh. The people of Kargil are mainly Muslims and noted for their orthodoxy (Fig. 3).

### Shergol

Between Kargil and Shergol one crosses the demarcation line between the Muslim and Buddhist areas. The small village of Shergol has tiny gompa perched halfway up the eastern slope of the mountain (Fig. 3).

### Mulbekh

This is a Buddhist village in which there are two gompas on the hillside above the village. Just beyond Mulbekh is a huge Chamba statue, an image of future Buddha, cut into the rock face beside the road.

### Lamayuru

From Mulbekh the road crosses the 3,718 m Namika La, passes through the large military encampment of Bodh Kharbu, the highest pass on the route. Lamayuru is the first of typical Ladakhi gompas perched on the hilltop with its village of the foot of the hill.

### Alchi

Alchi Gompa is unusual in that it is built on lowland, not perched on a hill-top. It is noted for its massive Buddha statues and lavish woodcarvings and artwork.

### Lekir and Basgo

Shortly after Saspur a steep road turns off the Lekir

Gompa which also has a monastery school. Close to Leh there is badly damaged fort at Basgo and the Basgo Gompa with interesting Buddha figures, although its wall painting have suffered much water damage.

### Leh

Situated about 10 km north-east of Indus River at an altitude of 3,540 m, Leh has a population of about 20,000 (1991). Centuries ago it was an important trading centre on the Old Carvan Silk-Route from China. Today, it is merely a military base and fascinating tourist centre.

Overlooking the town, perched on the Tsemo Hill, is the eight storeyed Leh Palace built by Singe Namgyal in the 16$^{th}$ century. Ladakh is known as the '*Abode of Gods*'. It has surreal landscape, meditative monks and benign people. It is one of the most attractive place for the cultural tourists and pleasure seekers.

### Monasteries in Ladakh

Spiritual life in Ladakh centres around monasteries, which served traders and travellers of yore as a place to stay. Each monastery is a conspicuous high building. The path leading to it is usually lined with prayer cylinder called *Chhoskor* which are made of metal and filled with prayer scrolls and charms. Before entering the monasteries a devotee sets the cylinder in motion with a gentle stroke, in the belief that he is sending to heaven prayers equal to the number in the cylinder, multiplied by the number of rotations.

Ladakh has about 5,000 lamas and a dozen main monasteries. Most of these can be conveniently visited from Leh as buses ply daily between these monasteries and Leh.

### Hemis Gompa

Ladakh's biggest monastery, Hemis Gompa is 49 km from Leh on the Leh-Manali Road. The monastery contains quite a few gold statues and Stupas decorated with precious stones. It is a superb collection of thankas including one which is supposed to be the largest in existence and is exhibited only once in 12 years. The next time it can be seen in 2004 A.D. The Hemis festival is held every year either in the second half of June or in the first half of July.

### Thinksey Gompa

Enroute to Hemis Gompa, the Thinksey Monastery provides a panoramic view of the green Indus valley from its vantage point a top a hill. It has chambers full of statues, stupas and thankes. There are 100 resident lamas and, allegedly, a nunnery. The Thinksey festival is held annually in early autumn.

### Shey Palace and Gompa

About 15 km from Leh towards the Hemis Gompa is the location of Shey Palace of the erstwhile Raja of Leh. Set upon a hill, and housing the largest golden topped victory stupa, the monastery has a two storeyed statue of sitting Buddha in copper and gold which leaves one breathless. Since the monastery is exclusive, it is preferable to make arrangements with the lama before visiting it.

### Shankar Gompa

Just 2 km from Leh is the location of Shankar Gompa. This monastery has a formidable collection of miniature statues of pure gold and a number of exciting paintings.

### Spituk Gompa

A few kilometres from Leh on the Srinagar-Leh Road, on a hilltop overlooking the Indus, the Spituk Monastery boasts not only some prized thankas, but a chamber with enormous statues of Kali Mata, whose faces are unveiled once a year during the Spituk Festival. The chamber contains an ancient collection of face masks too. Here the festival is held annually in winter.

### Phyang Gompa

The monastery of the red sect of the Buddhists, Phyang

Gompa lies 20 km short of Leh on the Srinagar-Leh Road. The monastery possesses some exquisite statues of thankas. Phyang festival is held during summer.

Apart from being the spiritual hub of all socio-economic activities, the monasteries are also the centres of Ladakh's cultural heritage. The religious fervour of the people finds expression in the annual festivals celebrated here. These festivals generally follow the lunar calender and therefore, their dates vary from year to year.[17] One of the festivals which is famous and celebrated with zest is the Hemis Festival. Hemis as stated above is the biggest monastery of Ladakh and the spiritual centre of Buddhists. People from all over Ladakh assemble here to attend this two day long festival. The festival is preceded by seven days of prayers by the monks in the monastery. The most impressive part of the festival is the famous mask dance which lamas of the monastery perform continuously for two days. The masks represent different gods and demons. The whole festival signifies the triumph of good over evil. The day marks the birthday of Guru Padmasambhava, the founder of the sect.

**Trekking in Ladakh**

Ladakh is a region providing enormous opportunities for the trekkers. While going on trekking the trekker should own a tent, a good sleeping bag, sufficient cotton and woollen clothing and some tinned food and juices. Essential medicines, ointments, lotions and creams for sunburns and chaffing would be useful. Use snow-goggles when in snow. Do not eat raw fruit and other eatables at market places. Drink as much liquid as possible and avoid excessive perspiration. It is best to avoid the consumption of alcohol. If you are a heart patient, consult your doctor before going. Respect the religious sanctity of monasteries as these are fountain heads of Buddhist religion and culture. Do not drink alcohol or smoke within a monastery, remove shoes before entering any of its chambers. Do not touch statues. Do not use photoflash inside a gompa as it is likely to damage the colour of the frescoes. Do not take photographs of bridges, strategic locations, military camps and installations as this is strictly prohibit.[18] Some of the important treks are as under.

### *Dras to Sanku*

This is a three-day trek into the Suru Valley, joining the Kargil-Padum Road at Sanku. It is an alternative route to the road down from Kargil.

### *Kargil to Padum*

It is seven-day trek from Kargil to Srinagar. When all bridges are open to route is accessible from early June to late October. The first day's travel is mainly on a surfaced road by bus to Parkchuk, after which one passes through Gulmatango pasture and Rangdhum Gompa. Beyond the Rangdum Gompa one has to cross the 4,401 m Pensi La (pass) into Zanskar proper. On the last day's walk from Phetoadum one crosses the river and passes by the Sam Gompa, one of the most important in Zanskar.

### *Padum to Lamayuru*

There are a number of alternatives for this trek from Padum into Ladakh, intersecting the road at Lamayuru, about half way from Kargil to Leh. The trek starts from Padum to Thonde, as on the short trek to the Zangla and Karsha Gompas. On day third, the difficult ascent to the 4,500 m Shing La Pass has to be made, but on day fourth the Nerag La (4,900 m) is even more difficult and local guide is a necessity. From Photosar, a small village, it is only two day's walk to Lamayuru. There is an alternative route from Photosar that takes a day longer. The alternative route from Padum starts out on the opposite side of the Zanskar river and takes you to the Linguist Gompa before joining up with the first tour on fifth day.

### **Padum to Kishtwar**

This trek into the southern part of Kashmir is not especially difficult although it crosses the 5,234 m Umasi La, which can only be done in fine weather. One can not use ponies on this trek but must take porters.

On the second day you reach the Zongkhul Gompa, which can also be visited on a short trek from Padum. Day 3 is a long climb and long descent over the snow-covered Umasi La. On day 4 you Zanskri porters will not continue further and you work with many ascents and descents but the road from Kishtwar, already extending to Galar, is gradually being lengthened.

Tourism is an age-old activity in the state, especially in the Valley of Kashmir. Innumerable tourists have visited the remote areas like Amarnath, Naranag, Awantipore and hill resorts like Pahalgam, Gulmarg and Bhadarwah from the time immemorial. During the Medieval period, the Mughal monarchs laid beautiful gardens (Nishat, Shalimar, Pari Mahal Chashma Shahi, Naseem Bagh etc.) around the Dal Lake. They utilized the natural springs, encarved cascades, cataracts and canals. They enriched the land with a variety of vegetation, flowers and orchards and revolutionized the handicrafts by encouraging the skilled workers. The traders and travellers for Yarkand (Central Asia) used to take rest in the valley during the Medieval period. A turning point in the history of tourism is marked by the construction of the Jammu-Srinagar National Highway No. 1 in 1948, previously known as the Banihal-Cart Road. With the Valley figuring on the air-map of the country in 1948, the international and domestic tourism received a great boost.

At present tourism is an important industry, attracting millions of peoples from all over the world. The tourists who visit the different cultural, religious, aesthetic and recreational places may be classified into : (i) domestic tourists who largely visit Vaishno Devi (Jammu) and Amarnath Caves (Kashmir), most of Indian tourists visit the Valley of Kashmir and their visits are generally confined to the summer and autumn seasons (May to October). The month of September and October in which the holidays of Durga Puja, Dussehra and Deepawali fall, provide a good opportunity to the domestic tourists to enjoy their holidays in the invigorating climate of the Valley of Kashmir and the tranquil setting of Jammu.

Contrary to this, the foreigners prefer to visit the Valley of Kashmir in the autumn and winter seasons, i.e., September to January. This is the period when in the hilly tracts of Jammu and Kashmir trekking and skiing are highly enjoyable.

**Table 10.1**
**Jammu and Kashmir : Tourists Coming to Kashmir Valley 1951-1995 ( in thousand)**

| S.No. | Year | Indian | Non-Indians | Total |
|---|---|---|---|---|
| 1. | 1951 | 9.33 | 1.25 | 10.58 |
| 2. | 1955 | 48.19 | 2.83 | 51.02 |
| 3. | 1960 | 63.37 | 11.19 | 74.56 |
| 4. | 1965 | 35.70 | 7.43 | 43.13 |
| 5. | 1970 | 131.50 | 11.50 | 143.00 |
| 6. | 1975 | 149.15 | 19.85 | 169.00 |
| 7. | 1980 | 548.49 | 46.03 | 594.52 |
| 8. | 1985 | 465.60 | 30.02 | 503.62 |
| 9. | 1990 | 6.10 | 4.62 | 10.72 |
| 10. | 1995 | 8.35 | 8.35 | – |

**Source:** Digest of Statistic 1993-1995, Jammu and Kashmir Govt. Directorate of Economics and Statistiscs, Srinagar.

The temporal growth pattern of tourists in the state has been given in Table 10.1. An Examination of Table 10.1 shows that in 1951 about 11,000 tourists visited the Valley of Kashmir, out of which 9,330 were domestic and 1,125 international tourists. With the passage of time the number of tourists grew substantially being 14.3 lakh in 1970. The influx of tourists was unparallel in 1980 when about 60 lakh tourists visited the Valley. Interestingly enough, there were 46,000 foreigner tourists who came to Kashmir in 1980. There however, occurred a slump in the number of tourists after 1989, the period when the militancy in the state increased and the Valley fell in to the grip of political turnmoil. In 1995, only 8,350 international tourists came in Kashmir. Under the prevailing political instability the domestic tourists did not venture to visit Kashmir. The sense of insecurity discouraged the pleasure seekers and nature enjoyers. In 2005 as per the official information the number of domestic as well as international tourists has increased. It is hoped that more number of tourists will be visiting the Valley in the years to come and this important industry will flourish again. The opening of the Srinagar-Muzaffarabad road will go a long way in the promotion of tourism in the Valley of Kashmir.

## International Tourists in Kashmir

The origin of foreign tourists in Kashmir can be traced back to Bernier, most probably the first European to enter the Valley of Kashmir. After him, innumerable number of tourists have visited the destination. In fact, over the period of time Kashmir has changed from a virgin beauty to a managed tourists attraction, the foreigners come in the valley with different purposes and motivations.

The countries and places of origin of the tourists who arrive in the Valley are as widespread as the globe itself.

In the beginning, Europeans formed the major proportion of the tourist who visited Kashmir. With the improvement in means of transportation and social amenities, Kashmir became more accessible and tourists from different parts of the world started pouring in. In fact, Kashmir attracts a substantial number of tourists from Australia, Austria, Belgium, Canada, Denmark, France, Germany, Hong Kong, Italy, Japan, Malaysia, Netherlands, New Zealand, Russia, South Africa, Spain, Switzerland, Sweden, U.K. and U.S.A. The other countries where from Kashmir is receiving tourists are : Afghanistan, Argentina, Bangladesh, China, Czechoslovakia, Egypt, Fiji, Finland, Hungary, Indonesia, Iran, Iraq, Ireland, Israel, Jordan, Kazakistan, Kenya, Labanon, Libya, Mauritius, Myanmar (Burma), Nepal, Norway, Pakistan, Poland, Russia, Saudi Arabia, Singapore, Tajakistan, Tanzania, Thailand, Turkmenistan, Uganda, Uzabaikistan, Venezuela, Yugoslavia, Bosnia, Zambia, etc.

The growth pattern of foreign tourists in the Valley of Kashmir has been given in Table 10.2.

**Table 10.2**
**Jammu and Kashmir : Temporal increase in Foreign Tourists–1986-1994**

| Year | No. of Foreign Tourists | Increase/Decrease |
|---|---|---|
| 1986 | 54,118 | – |
| 1987 | 49,468 | +6,050 |
| 1988 | 59,938 | +700 |
| 1989 | 67,776 | +7,838 |
| 1990 | 4,627 | –63,149 |
| 1991 | 4,886 | +259 |
| 1992 | 9,339 | +4,453 |
| 1993 | 8,026 | –1,313 |
| 1994 | 15,296 | +7,270 |

**Source:** Dept. of Tourism, Jammu and Kashmir, Srinagar.

An examination of Table 10.2 shows that over 53,000 foreigners visited the Valley of Kashmir in 1986 which rose to 67,800 in 1989. There occurred a phenomenal decrease in the foreign tourists in 1990 in which only 4,600 tourists from abroad arrived in the Valley. The main cause of this tremendous decrease was the *Azadi* Movement, which led to chaos, militancy and insecurity. This downward trend in the arrival of tourists continued upto 1992. In 1992 only 9,300 tourists came to the Valley while this number increased to 15,300 in 1994. After the partition of the subcontinent, it was 1989 when the maximum number of international tourists (67,800) visited the Valley, when 1990 recorded the lowest number of foreigners, being only about 4,600. The substantial decrease in the number of foreign tourists affected the economy of the state adversely and created many economic and occupational problems for the people. In fact, many of the workers who were dependent on tourism have to change their occupations. The business people and the landless workers had to out migrate from the valley.

**Table 10.3**
**Kashmir Valley : Number of Foreign Tourists (countrywise) (in thousand)**

| S.No. | Country | 1971 | 1981 | 1991 | 1993 |
|---|---|---|---|---|---|
| 1. | U.K. | 2.10 | 6.89 | 0.57 | 0.87 |
| 2. | West Germany/Germany | NA | 4.28 | 0.48 | 0.74 |
| 3. | Italy | 0.36 | 1.54 | 0.59 | 0.61 |
| 4. | France | 1.45 | 5.35 | 0.50 | 0.43 |
| 5. | U.S.A. | 5.63 | 7.44 | 0.24 | 0.41 |
| 6. | Australia | 0.73 | 2.98 | 0.33 | 0.37 |
| 7. | Sweden | 0.07 | 0.21 | 0.13 | 0.27 |
| 8. | Switzerland | 0.42 | 0.93 | 0.20 | 0.26 |
| 9. | Japan | 0.68 | 1.26 | 0.19 | 0.21 |
| 10. | Spain | 0.03 | 2.28 | 0.10 | 0.20 |
| 11. | Belgium | 0.14 | 0.69 | 0.07 | 0.19 |
| 12. | Malaysia | 0.18 | 0.54 | 0.04 | 0.17 |
| 13. | Canada | 0.43 | 1.36 | 0.12 | 0.15 |
| 14. | New Zealand | 0.08 | 0.79 | 0.10 | 0.10 |
| 15. | Netherlands | 0.37 | 0.82 | 0.03 | 0.08 |
| 16. | U.S.S.R./Russia | 0.03 | 0.40 | 0.1 | |
| 17. | S. Africa | 0.35 | 1.14 | 0.03 | 0.05 |
| 18. | Iran | 0.07 | 1.01 | | |
| 19. | Others | 2.11 | 6.12 | 1.17 | 2.91 |
| | Total | 15.24 | 46.03 | 4.89 | 8.03 |

**Source:** *Digest of Statistics*, Jammu and Kashmir; 1993-94, Directorate of Economics and Statistics, Srinagar.

The major countries from where the foreigners visit the Kashmir have been given in Table 10.3.

The maximum number of tourists in 1981 came from U.S.A. (7,440), followed by U.K. 6,890. France, Germany, Australia, Spain, Japan and Italy are the other countries from where a sizeable number of tourists visit Kashmir.

The bulk of the tourists in Kashmir is domestic. The two cultural and religious sites, i.e., Vaishno Devi and Amarnath Caves attract a large number of tourists form the Hindu Belt, comprising the states of Bihar, Chhattisgarh, Himachal

Pradesh, Jharkhand, Madhya Pradesh, Rajasthan and Uttar Pradesh. The Bengalis, Punjabis, Gujaratis, Maharashtrian, etc. visit the Valley of Kashmir mainly during the Durga Puja and Dussehera holidays in the months of September, October and November. The data available from the Directorate of Tourism, Jammu and Kashmir (given in Table 10.4) show that in 1960-61 only 400 pilgrims visited the Amarnath Cave. Despite political instability and militancy, more and more number of people are visiting Amarnath. It shows a revival of Shivaits Hinduism.

An analysis of Table 10.4 vividly shows that in 1950-51 Vaishno Devi was an insignigicant pilgrimage place attracting only 300 of pilgrims. In 1960-61 about 1,600 people made *yatra* to Vaishno Devi while this figure reached to 21,690 in 1990-91 and 33,690 in 1993-94. The phenomenal increase in the number of devotees and their pilgrimage to Vaishno Devi show that Hindu fundamentalism is on the increase and it is not the rural folk alone from northern India who perform pilgrimage to Vaishno Devi, the urban educated, rich and elites are increasingly going on *yatra* to this sacred place. The improved condition of staying and resting facilities developed on the way have made this difficult journey, easy to perform. Even the aged people and children may be seen making *yatra* to Vaishno Devi. Consequently, the number of visitors is increasing at a faster pace. More social amenities and infrastructural facilities need to be developed to make the journey easier for the fast growing number of visitors to the shrine.

The number of people visiting the Vaishno Devi has been given in Table 10.4

**Table 10.4**
**Jammu and Kashmir : Tourists Visiting Vaishno Devi and Amarnath Cave, 1950-2001 (in 000')**

| S.No. | Year | Amarnath Cave | Vaishno Devi |
|---|---|---|---|
| 1. | 1950-51 | NA | 0.03 |
| 2. | 1955-56 | NA | 0.06 |

| | | | |
|---|---|---|---|
| 3. | 1960-61 | 0.04 | 1.60 |
| 4. | 1965-66 | 0.07 | 2.30 |
| 5. | 1975-76 | 0.08 | 5.81 |
| 6. | 1980-81 | 0.02 | 12.13 |
| 7. | 1985-86 | 0.42 | 14.85 |
| 8. | 1990-91 | 0.05 | 21.69 |
| 9. | 1993-94 | 0.56 | 33.69 |
| 10. | 2000-01 | 0.65 | 42.15 |

**Source:** Directorate Tourism, Jammu and Kashmir.

Tourism is a composite industry. It consists of various segments which can produce a wide range of products and services. Many of these services often not physically measurable. There is also nothing like a standard tourism product. These features of tourism industry make the task of measuring its economic impact a highly complex subject.

The economic benefits of tourism are mainly identified as : (i) foreign exchange earning, (ii) income creation, (iii) employment generation, (iv) contribution to state revenue, and (v) regional development, improved income distribution and multiplier effect, promotion of international economic cooperation, capitalisation of national resources, stimulation of national entrepreneurship, improvement of transport infrastructure are some of the other benefits of tourism. Many of these effects are, however, not directly measurable particularly in-view of yawning data-gaps in the tourism sector.

Tourism is also having many social consequences. These include (i) social integration (ii) widening of social opportunities, (iii) awakening of awareness of national entity, (iv) reviving and strengthening of cultural heritage, (v) strengthening of international understanding, (vi) projection of national image abroad, (vii) spread of awareness of world affairs, etc.

Lack of scientific planning and decision in the promotion of tourism is also having economic and social costs. In the economic front, it may lead to inflation and scarcity of essential items. The social costs are more serious and irrevocable. These include social and environmental pollution, drug trafficking and flesh trade, corruption of moral and cultural values etc. Tourism promotion plan of any country has to be, therefore, consistent with its social, economic, ecological and political systems.

## Economic Consequences of Tourism

Tourism is often viewed as a new wave of economic opportunity and is largely responsible for the transfer of wealth from one nation to another and redistribution of income, leading to the gross increase in income in the host community of tourism region. The degree of benefit from tourism however, depends largely upon the level of self-sufficiency of the economy of hosting region. In recent years tourism has been considered as a great transformer of economic change. Consequently, tourism has been considered as an industry. Moreover, tourism which is basically a labour intensive industry proves a resist the pressure of economic recession of nations and combat regional imbalances and economic crunch in regional economy.

It is difficult task to assess the impact of tourism on the economy of the concerned society. Tourism, however, influences the economy in two ways, i.e., (i) the broad consumption items, e.g., transport, accommodation, drinks and shopping services which have a direct effect, and (ii) the links between the trades directly involved in tourism which supply the tourism trade with goods and services. The full impact of tourism on economy is not just through expenditure on the tourist trade, it embraces of those industries which involve the process to supply goods and services. In the opinion of Smith, each time a tourist makes an expenditure, a ripple of additional spending is sent through the economy which is known as the multiplier effect.

It is well known that tourism generates employment. The development of tourism enhance wages, salaries, rent interest and profits. Since tourism is labour intensive, the greatest proportion of income comes from wages and salaries. In remote tourist sites like Doda, Kishtwar, Bhaderwah : Sonmarg, Daksum, Gulmarg, Pahalgam, Aharbal, Kargil, Leh, Rang-dum, Parkchak, Mulbek, etc. it is the only dominant economic activity that yields good income to the people. Taxation on tourist activity also yields income to the state government. Taxes on hotel bills clubs, wine-shops and entry tickets to parks and museums, etc. raise additional income to the government.

Tourism provides employment of thousands of people in the state of Jammu and Kashmir who work in hotels, houseboats, guest houses, restaurant dormitories, dak-bungalows, holiday inns and tent houses.

In addition to employment in the tertiary sector, tourism encourages the development of handicrafts and household industries. The state of Jammu and Kashmir, especially the Valley of Kashmir has always enjoyed a universal fame for the exquisite quality and novelty of its arts and crafts. Travellers, poets and historians have paid glowing tributes to the skill, dexterity and craftsmanship of Kashmiris. Industries like carpet-making, fur, leather and embroidery works, papier-mache and woodcarving, willow works, silk manufacturing, pottery-making etc. employ a large number of handicrafts and household industries in the state of Jammu and Kashmir.

Transport is the lifeline of tourist in the state. Rock carving cutting and building and rock blasting and landslide clearing activities provide employment to a large number of people. Moreover, circulatory systems like roads, treks, rope-ways and waterways need enormous labour force for their construction and maintenance. Over 50,000 of skilled and unskilled workers derive their livelihood from these activities who would have been rendered unemployed in the state. Tourism discourage outward migration of labour and attract immigrants. This process strengthens the economy of the state.

In addition to job opportunities, tourism accelerates the souvenir making industry. Moreover, a large number of pony-keepers, taxi drivers, *shikarawalas*, boatmen, helpers, tourist guides, shopkeepers, vendors, and fruit sellers directly depend on tourist industry.

Tourism has thus, opened a new vista for the regional development in the state of Jammu and Kashmir. In the remote tourist sites away from the urban centre a kind of micro-urbanization has to take place as a consequence of tourists demands. The construction of hotels, guest houses, roads, bridges, railway lines, electricity and gas supplies, sanitation, telecommunication network and host of things are developed to provide the required infrastructural facilities to the tourists.

Tourism is a rich source of earning foreign exchange. International tourists generally buy services from the region/ state and therefore, pay for invisible.

**Adverse Effects of Tourism on Economy**

Despite all these merits heavy rush of tourists in the state instigates numerous socio-economic evils. Some of such vices have been briefly given in the following paragraphs.

1. Development of tourism and influx of foreign tourists lead to inflation. Wealthy tourists having a superior purchasing power result into price rise which may by beyond the affordable limits of most of the local population. The cost of living in the areas of attraction for international tourists goes up substantially.
2. Tourism development lead to phenomenal increase in the land prices especially in the areas of attraction for foreign tourists. For example, in the period between 1955 to 1999 the price of land along the boulevard (Srinagar) has gone up by about 1000 times. To be more specific the price of land along the Boulevard in 1955 was about Rs. 5 per sq. yard which rose to Rs. 10,000 per sq. yard in 1998. Similarly, the price of land in Gulmarg and Pahalgam has recorded a stupendous increase being Rs. 1 per sq.

yard in 1955 and Rs. 500 and Rs. 600 at Gulmarg and Pahalgam in 1998 respectively.

3. Tourism in the state of Jammu and Kashmir is largely a seasonal activity. Its seasonal character causes seasonal unemployment in winters and shortage of workers during the peak summer season. The hotels and tourists accommodations remain underutilized during the lean season which is a share wastage of the resources. The seasonality of tourism also forces the labourers to outmigrate in search of jobs which puts great stress on the migrants from the state.
4. The promotion of tourism generally creates undue stress on a developing economy. The tourists expect high standards, the provision of which may upset domestic priorities, creating jealousy and discontent.
5. The non-judicious and disproportional use of land and increase in land price convert small farmers into landless labourers. Small farmers dispose off their tiny holdings for more profit. Ultimately, more labour force is generated with leads to unemployment and discontent among.
6. The native population suffers while the tourists enjoy the social amenities. In the development planning of the state there should be more emphasis on the development of basic amenities, like roads, electricity, school, hospitals and public transport. Contrary to this preference is given to the construction of hotels and recreational centres. Consequently, the outsiders enjoy life while the local people suffer.
7. Tourism hinders the establishment and growth of the productive industries. In fact, tourism diverts scare capital away from industries and agriculture.

## Social Implications of Tourism

Tourism is a socio-cultural event for the tourists and the hosts. It plays a vital role in social change and brings gradual and radical changes in the cultural values and traditions of the people. The impact is, however, more marked in the lesser developed societies of the developing countries. Tourism often has significant cultural implications (restoration of historical and archaelogical monuments), social and political understanding.

According to a study conducted by the UNESCO, the relationship between hosts and guests in the destination areas can be characterized by five main features : (i) they involve transitory relationship. Tourists come to a place or region for a short-period, so an interaction between hosts and guests has little chance to progress beyond casual and superficial level, (ii) there are spatial and temporal constraints to visitor-host integration. The hospitality, business, often becomes exploitative to take the advantage of the seasonal character of tourism here. Tourism facilities and services are concentrated in a few locations, (iii) the visitor resident meetings lack the spontaneity associated with individual schedules. Package tours, planned interactions and scheduled meetings may be arranged but these are only controlled events and finally become commercial in nature, (iv) the meeting and visitors and residents is general an unequal and unbalanced experience. Residents often feel inferior when they compare their situation to a visitor's apparent wealth, (v) while the visitor is on a holiday-making mood enjoying novel experience, for the resident such events and meeting have become routine without any fun. The social consequences of tourism have been briefly described in the following paragraphs.

## 1. Transformation in Lifestyle

The dwellers of the hilly and mountainous state of Jammu and Kashmir are generally tradition loving, conservative people. They respect their cultural value appreciably. The society has, however, transformed in the areas of tourists interest. There is strong preference of the rich people for the luxury and foreign good. The presence of tourists make the society more liberal and tolerant. Tourism also reduce suspicion and exclusiveness among the hosts and the guests.

## 2. International Understanding

Travel helps to broaden the mental horizon of man. Tourists in the Jammu and Kashmir state gain an insight into the customs, traditions and way of life of the people, and home, the feeling that man is one is human society. It leads to world peace and promotes international understanding. Tourism can be the best remedy to curb insurgence and violence in the state as it draws people and nations closer to each other. It may help to dissipate prejudice and correct misunderstanding.

## 3. Cultural Exchange

A tourist arrives with treasure of his civilization and history of his country of which he is an ambassador. Travel and tourism is the best way for establishing a special unwritten and unspoken relationship with people of different countries and different times having different modes of life. Thus, tourism promotes cultural exchange and cultural enrichment of those who travel as well those who are the hosts. When a tourist comes in contact with the place he visits and its population, a social exchange takes place. His social background affects the social structure and mode of life of his destination. He in turn is affected by it and many a times carries back home new habits and ways of life. The culture of a destination attracts people of architecture and historical monuments. Moreover, festivals and exhibitions rely heavily on visitors for their audience and attendence. The educational and cultural significance of tourism implicit in seeing people and living a different exciting life which help to tie the chord of eternal human friendship. Tourism is an education of other peoples habits, food, dress and the gamut of life. It, thus, contributes to the mutual knowledge of man and to the development of sense of hospitality. Tourism has made Jammu and Kashmir known to different corners of the world.

## 4. Tourism is the Repository of Cultural Heritage

Tourism has been increasingly recognized for its role in saving many of the world's cultural treasures. In Jammu and

Kashmir, tourism brings good revenue and helps the government in maintaining archaeological sites. For example, Parihaspora, Pandrathan, Martand, Takht-e-Sulaiman (Shankaracharya), Pari Mahal, Vaishno Devi. Weaving and woodcarving in the ancient style have been rejuvenated.

### 5. Tourism and Infrastructural Development

Tourism helps in the development of social amenities. All the hill station and cultural sites are well connected with metalled roads, post, telegraph and telephone services. The power and water supply are also more regular in the places of tourism interest. With the improvement of these social amenities the rural products (fresh fruits and vegetables) have quick access to the markets.

### 6. Tourism and Change in Housing Design

Tourism has significantly influenced the design of architecture in the state of Jammu and Kashmir. With increase in resort housing, hotels and guest house have been designed and contracted in a planned way. In Srinagar the new colonies like Raj Bagh, Kursoo, Rawalpora, Shivpora, Shah Faisal Colony, Berin and Hyderpora and in Jammu, colonies like Gandhi Nagar, Shastri Nagar etc. have been constructed on the new patterns with R.C.C. structures. Unfortunately, the growth of slums in Jammu and Srinagar cities are also because of influx of labourers who are pulled in the region by the forces of tourism.

### 7. Promotion to Local Arts and Crafts

Tourism is one of the significant factors which keeps arts and crafts of the underdeveloped and developing societies alive. In the state of Jammu and Kashmir, tourism is a blessing for the local and regional handicrafts, music, woodwork, carpentry, papier mache and shawl-making. The arts and crafts speak of the grammer of Kashmiri society and act as its representative in the outside world. The scenic splendour and aesthetics of Jammu and Kashmir is reflected specimens of art and handicrafts.

## Adverse Effect of Tourism

Despite all these merits of tourism, it has many adverse effects on the society. For example, cultural pollution, deterioration in morality and increase in the rate of crimes.

1. The introduction and imitation of foreign ways of life in the developing societies living in isolation and relative isolation bring about change in attitudes, values and social behaviour of the people. Unfortunately, the younger generation is the most susceptible to the pressure of the demonstration effect created by tourists. The youths attempt to imitate the lifestyle of visiting tourists. Glimpses of copied western culture may be seen in the popularity of jeans, western pop music and rock dance. As the two culture come into contact, the local values get transformed, ultimately leading to culture pollution.
2. The second setback occurs in the form of commercialization of art. Tourists seek local artifacts as souvenirs. The heavy demand for typical artifacts leads to bulk production for the poorly crafted works (referred to as 'airport-art').
3. Close proximity and interaction with tourists influence the food habits of those who are associated with tourist industry, e.g. guides *Shikarawalas*, taxi operators, houseboat owners, pony-keepers and people working in hotels and guest houses. Some of these workers have indulged in gambling delinquecy and narcotic drug-trafficking. It is generally believed that tourists are largely responsible for increase in liquor consumption, drug-addiction and smoking in the region. The morality has loosened and some of the youngsters are becoming increasingly permissive in their behaviour, reading morally disgusting literature and enjoying obscene films and club life. Consequently, the age-old sound cultural fabric has been threatened and the society feels frustrated. If these negative impacts of tourism are not checked the cultural ethos of the people of Jammu and Kashmir will be damaged beyond reparation.

## Impact of Tourism on Ecology

Tourism is essentially a service industry, depending almost entirely on natural ingredients like aesthetic beauty of mountains, hills, lakes, waterbodies, sylvan canopy, flora, fauna and bracing climate. Tourism is however, not a less polluting industry. It has increasingly been recognized as one of the most polluting industries. Some of the influence of tourism on ecology and environment have been concisely presented in the following paragarphs.

### 1. *Damage to the Natural Environment*

With the increase of population and urbanization, the number of tourists is increasingly year after year. It is leading to physical deterioration of environment. There is an imbalance between tourist demand and physical carrying capacity of the area offering tourist activity. Under such circumstances the expected symbiotic relationship between tourism and conservation breaks down resulting into ecological crisis.

### 2. *Pollution*

Tourism-generated pollution is now a threat in the state of Jammu and Kashmir. Tourism has brought with it overcrowding, congestion, traffic snarls in places like Srinagar, Jammu, Pahalgam, Gulmarg, Sonmarg, Vaishno Devi, etc. The meadows of Gulmarg and Sonmarg have been trampled, the Dal, Wular, Aanchar and Gangabal lakes have been polluted. The waterbodies, the scenic spots, the margs (alpine pastures), the natural springs, glaciers, outwash plains and trekking routes have been degraded largely because of the undisciplined and careless behaviour of the tourists.

The Valley of Kashmir has been considered as a powerful magnet for tourists. It caters to the needs of every type of tourists. Its physiographic, orographic and stratigraphic setting is most attractive but ecologically fragile. The unplanned and unregulated tourism has created many environmental problems in the region.

### *3. Pollution of Waterbodies*

The state of Jammu and Kashmir, especially the Valley of Kashmir is characterized with some beautiful lakes. The ecosystem of these lakes is degrading fast. The Dal Lake of Srinagar, well known for its geographical setting and splendid beauty, is in a pathetic condition. Its crystal-clear water has become highly polluted, giving an obnoxious odour. It has become the victim of eutrophication, situation, encroachment, vegetables cultivation in floating fields, and sewage disposal. It is not only that its water-covered area is shrinking and it is becoming shallower the quality of its water is one of the worst in the Himalayan region. Wrapers, plastic bags, tins, cans, rage, vegetables peeling, empty cigarette cases, garbage and numerous weeds may be seen, floating in its water affecting the look of the lake.

The area of Dal Lake which was 22 sq. km in 1931 has shrunk to only about 15 sq. km in 1999. Out of the present area of the Dal Lake only 11 sq. km contains water. In order to accommodate more tourists in their house in boats and houses, more and more *Hanjis* are settling in and around the lake.[21]

In the mid-1970s with tourism becoming a key industry for Jammu and Kashmir, the pressure on the lake multiplied. There were less than a hundred houseboats on the Dal and Nagin lakes at the turn of the century, but their number grew to a staggering 1,400 by 1981. The 1981 census recorded that hamlets around the lake had a population of 24,500, an increase of over cent percent since 1973. About 5,000 people were found to be the permanently residents on the houseboats. Although the tourists population dwindled after *Mujahadeen* violence broke out in 1989, the human population on and around the lake registered a steady growth. The Lakes and Water Development Authority (LWDA) believes that about 45,000 people are now residents on the houseboats and hamlets, and assuming just about 5,000 tourists live on them through the year, the lake bore the burden of about 5,000 people.

The heavy deforestation in the catchment of Dachingam and Telbal Nallah, which discharge their water into the Dal Lake have accentuated the process of siltation. According to one estimate, the Dal Lake bears an annual silt load of about 80,000 tonnes. Such of the silt is deposited near its northern shore as it is blocked by a Bund (embankment) in the Lake. The land, thus, formed has been reclaimed for farming and pastoral activity. The run-off from the fertilized paddy fields and untreated sewage work as excellent manures leading to much faster growth of weeds and eutrification in the lake. The stories of Wular, Anchar and Manasbal lakes are almost identical. Tourism development has, thus, damaged the lakes ecosystems making them less useful for the people.

### 4. *Landslides*

The heavy vehicular traffic on the National Highway No.1 (Jammu Srinagar Road) is one of the main causes of landslides between Batote and Ramban (Nashri area), between Ramban and Ramsu (Fagla Tract) and between Banihal and Qazigund, Similarly, the low altitudinal zones Gulmarg, Pahalgam, Sonmarg, Kishtwar, Bhadarwah, Doda, Kargil, Leh, Udhampur, Rajouri and Poonch experience a large number of landslides every year.

### *References*

1. Johnston, R.J., 1990, '*The Dictionary of Human Geography*', B. Blackwell Ltd. Oxford, U.K.
2. Christaller, W., 1964, '*Some Consideration of Tourism Location in Europe*', Pap. Reg. Sci. Assoc. 12, pp. 95-105.
3. Husain, M., 2002, '*Systematic Geography of Jammu and Kashmir*', Rawat Publications, 2000.
4. Johnston, R.J., op. cit., p. 492.
5. Robinson, H., 1976, '*A Geography of Tourism*', Mac Donal and Evans, London, xxi.
6. Murphy, R.E., 1985, '*Tourism : A Community Approach*', Routledge, New York.
7. *WTO News*, August, 1990.
8. *Report prepared by the U.S.A. based Wharton Econometric forecasting.*

9. *Associates (WEFA).*
10. Garrison, 1989, *WTO Projections.*
11. Crowther, G., et.al., 1990, '*India : A Travel Survival Kit*', Lonely planet Pub. Hawthorn, Australia.
12. Ibid, p. 239.
13. Ibid.
14. Ibid.
15. Ibid.
16. Ibid.
17. *Department of Tourism,* Jammu and Kashmir, Ladakh, 1986.
18. Ibid.
19. Faried, A., 1998, '*Tourism in Kashmir Valley and its impact on Ecology, Economy and Society*', unpublished Ph.D. Thesis, Jamia Millia Islamia, New Delhi.
20. Ibid.
21. Smith, S., 1983, '*Recreation Geography*', London.
22. Swami, P., '*To Save a Lake*', Frontline, June 5, 1998, pp. 66-70.

## Chapter-XI

# Transport and Trade

Development of cheap and efficient means of transport and communications are the prerequisite for the speedy and balanced economic growth. Without an effective network of means of transport and communications, the natural endowment of a region cannot be exploited judiciously. The development of transport, however, depends on physical, historical, technological, economic and political factors.

Transportation involves movement of goods, persons, letters, newspapers as well as the non-physical transfer of information by phone, radio, telex, wireless etc. In brief, transport and communications involve the transfer of people, commodities and information over space. This transfer takes place along a line of communication between two places.

Transportation has always been an important activity of man from the most primitive to the most developed states of the world. It is both a result and a cause of an advancing society. The potential of a country and its transportation determined largely by mountains, terrain, nature of rocks, swamps deserts and thick forests. Such topographic features stretching across mainlines of trade and travel serve as obstacles to land surface transportation. Moreover, socio-cultural and ecopolitical factors also exert great influence in the develeopment of nation's transportation. In fact, commercial land industrial growth stimulates invention and innovation in agriculture, mining and manufacturing which tend to increase demand for transportation. Apart from development of the region, transportation plays a critical role in times of national emergency like war, famines and other natural calamities. Good means of transport and communications are thus necessary for the very existence of a nation.

The State of Jammu and Kashmir is essentially mountainous in character excepting the plains of Jammu and the Jhelum Valley of Kashmir Division. Development of railways through difficult terrains is not only stupendous task, it may be uneconomic and difficult to maintain. The state was brought on the Railway Map in 1970 when jammu was connected with Pathankot. The total length of railway line in the state at present is about 80 kms. Apart from Jammu Tawi, Bari-Brahman, Vijainagar, Jammu, Samba, Chagwal, Hiranagar, Chak-Dayala, Chhan-Arorian, Budhi and Kathua are the railway stations in the State on the Jammu-Pathankot Railway Line. Efforts are also being made to connect Udhampur with Jammu construction work has been started and it is hoped that the railway line between these two stations will be completed by the end of 2002. Extension of this railway line beyond Udhampur is difficult owing to the steep Pir-Panjals and weak rock formations between Batote and Ramban-known as *Nashiri*, which is often affected adversely by landslides and avalanches. Development of railway line between Jammu and Pathankot has, however, helped appreciably in the movement of passengers and goods. This railway line is adequately coping with the demand of the region and especially helping in clearing the rush of pilgrims who visit Vaishno Devi near Katra in the Jammu Division. The Valley of Kashmir which is levelled, highly fertile and densely populated also deserves a network of railway lines.

## Roads

In a mountainous state like Jammu & Kashmir over fifty percent of which is almost barren and uninhabited, roads play a vital role in the transportation of people and goods. The state in general and the Valley of Kashmir in particular has throughout its long history functioned and propered as the main focal centre. The Central Asian Trade Route, connecting the Subcontinent with Yarkand, Khotan, Tashkant, Samarkand, Balkh, Bukhara, Ashikabad, Baku, Azerbaijan and Georgia debouched on to it through the Sindh Valley (a tributary of Jhelum) and the Indus River. The Jhelum was also an important transport artery. The Jammu-Srinagar-Leh National Highway (No. 1-A), the Jammu-Poonch Highway and a number of state roads radiating in all directions have revolutionized the transport of the state. In other words, roads provide the most fundamental mode of transport in the State. The roads connect all the 56 towns and cities (Chapter 6) of Jammu, Kashmir and Ladakh Divisions. Moreover, there are roads connecting, towns, villages, factories, farms and mines which provide the required feeder service. In the state, over 80% of surface transport is carried on by roads, while in the Kashmir and Ladakh Divisions roads carry almost 100% of people and passengers.

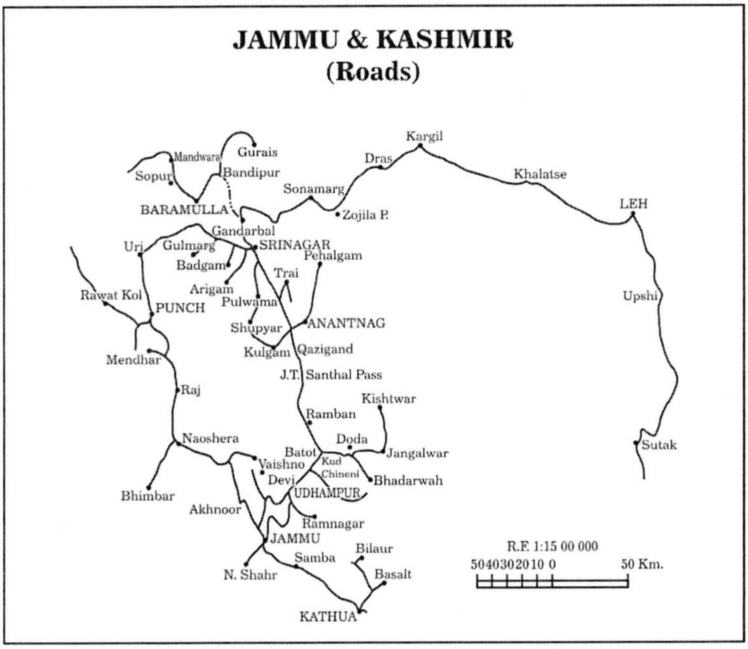


**Fig. 20 : Jammu & Kashmir–Roads**

The National Highway No. 1-A, i.e., Pathankot, Jammu, Srinagar, Uri and Srinagar, Kargil, Leh is maintained by the Borders Development Board. Since the road has been carved out through the weak sedimentary and metamorphic formations, especially between Batote and Ramban (*Nashiri* area) its maintenance is quite expensive. During winters, snow and at the occurrence of snow and rains, heavy landslides occur and parts of the National Highway slip into the mighty Chenab River. The Nashiri By-Pass (Neera to Batote) however, provides some relief if there is landslide between Batote and the Chenab Main Bridge. As a result of landslides the Kashmir and Ladakh Divisions temporarily remain cut off from the rest of the country. In winters when the supply of vegetables cereals, kersosene, and sheep is disrupted owing to road blocked, the people of these Divisions have tough time and life in the valley becomes miserable.

The Border Roads Organisation has also constructed one of the world's highest road from Manali (Himachal Pradesh) to Leh (Ladakh). The average altitude of the terrain over which this road passes varies 4,857 to 5,485 metres. The road has considerably reduced the distance between Chandigarh and Ladakh.

In Jammu and Kashmir there are a number of state highways. These are the main arteries of trade and commerce, and passenger transport from one division to another and from one town to another. The maintenance of these roads is the state responsibility. The spatial distribution of roads, and their lengths have been in Table 11.1.

**Table 11.1**
**Roads–Jammu & Kashmir State, 1984.**

| District | Area Sq. km. | Road Length (km.) | One Km. of Road per sq. km. |
|---|---|---|---|
| **Kashmir Division** | | | |
| 1. Anantnag | 3,984 | 1,199 | 3.32 |
| 2. Badgam | 1,371 | 633 | 2.15 |

| | | | |
|---|---|---|---|
| 3. Baramulla | 4,588 | 1,140 | 4.02 |
| 4. Kupwara | 2,379 | 556 | 4.27 |
| 5. Srinagar | 2,228 | 814 | 2.73 |
| 6. Pulwama | 1,398 | 724 | 1.93 |
| **Jammu Division** | | | |
| 7. Doda | 11,691 | 627 | 18.64 |
| 8. Jammu | 3,097 | 1,267 | 2.44 |
| 9. Kathua | 2,651 | 624 | 4.25 |
| 10. Poonch | 1,674 | 125 | 13.39 |
| 11. Rajouri | 2,630 | 354 | 7.42 |
| 12. Udhampur | 4,550 | 547 | 8.31 |
| **Ladakh Division** | | | |
| 13. Kargil | 14,036 | 454 | 30.91 |
| 14. Leh | 82,665 | 578 | 143.02 |
| Total | 1,35,942 | 9,644 | 28.81 |

**Source:** Digest of Statistics, J & K, 1984.

The Central and the State Governments have shown appreciable interest in the development of National, State and District Roads. The condition of most of the state and district roads leaves much to desire. The spatial distribution of road is highly uneven. The total length of road is 3644 kms (Table 11.1) and on the average there is 1 km metalled road after 29 kms. The plain areas have dense road network, while the hilly and mountainous settlements are not well connected by roads. The districts of Pulwama, Badgam, Srinagar and Jammu have one km. road after every 2.75 sq. km. area. The levelled topography and dense population of these districts have helped in the development of an elaborate network of roads as the construction and maintenance of roads under such geographical condition is easy and cheap. In the districts of Anantnag, Baramulla, Kupwara, Kathua and Rajouri which have partly hilly and partly plain areas about 7 sq. km. or less area has one km. of road. Contrary to this the hilly districts of Leh, Kargil, Doda and Poonch have very poor network of roads. In Leh one km. of metalled road is available after every 143 sq. km. and in Kargil after every 40 sq. kms. while in Doda on the average every 19 sq. kms. of area has one km. of road (Table 11.1). These districts have rugged and mountainous topography and are the most sparsely populated. An analysis of Table 11.1 shows that only a few districts have dense network of roads. The development and maintenance of the district roads (connecting towns and large villages with the district headquarters) is not satisfactory. Many of them at places are unsurfaced and are without culverts and bridges. Extension and proper maintenance of state and district roads are imperative for all round economic development. Agricultural marketing will particularly improve with the development of these roads.

The total number of vehicles on roads in the state in 1983-84 was about 25,915. The number and frequency of buses, trucks, taxis, cars, jeeps, auto-rickshaws, scooters vary from road to road, depending on the demand of population and goods. The Jammu Srinagar National Highway (No. 1-A) is however, one of the most busy routes of the country. On the average about 800 buses (public and private) and trucks pass through the Banihal Toll Post everyday. This number varies from summer to winter months. For example, in winters occassionally the road is closed under the impacts of ice, snow and heavy rains which may cause landslides in the *Nashiri* Tract and the traffic may remain suspended, while during the summer season upto 2000 buses and trucks may pass through the Jawahar-Tunnel. The temporal growth in the traffic on the Jammu-Srinagar National Highway has been given in Table 11.2.

**Table 11.2**
**Traffic passed through Banihal Toll Post Vehicles coming Jammu to Srinagar**

| Year | Buses/Trucks | Others | Total |
|---|---|---|---|
| 1951 | 16,000 | – | 16,000 |
| 1961 | 46,000 | 2,000 | 48,000 |
| 1971 | 78,000 | 8,000 | 86,000 |
| 1981 | 1,23,000 | 15,000 | 1,38,000 |
| 1984 | 1,27,000 | 15,000 | 1,32,000 |

**Source:** J & K, Transport Deptt. Srinagar, 1984.

An examination of Table 11.2 reveals that in 1951 only 16,000 vehicles (buses and trucks) entered the Kashmiri Division from the Jammu Division which rose to 1,32,000 in 1984. In fact, the construction of Jawahar-Tunnel has provided a great stimulus for the transportation of people and goods between Jammu and Srinagar. The vehicles going from Srinagar to Jammu have been given in Table 11.3.

**Table 11.3**
**Vehicles going from Srinagar to Jammu, 1984**

| Year | Buses/Trucks | Others | Total |
|---|---|---|---|
| 1951 | 16,000 | – | 16,000 |
| 1961 | 45,000 | 3,000 | 48,000 |
| 1971 | 73,000 | 3,000 | 76,000 |
| 1981 | 1,26,000 | 19,000 | 1,45,000 |
| 1984 | 1,21,000 | 15,000 | 1,36,000 |

**Source:** J & K, Transport Deptt. Srinagar, 1984.

In 1984 about 1.36 lakh vehicles passed through the Jawahar Tunnel from Kashmir Division to Jammu Division. Out of the total vehicles 1.21 lakh were buses and trucks and 15 thousand taxis and others. Table 11.3 further shows that there is a phenominal increase in the traffic, passed through the Banihal Toll Post, the maximum vehicles passed being 1.38 in 1981. This year was politically most stable which attracted a large number of tourists in the Valley. With the passage of time the flow of traffic is expected to increase stupendously. To cope with the situation it is imperative to expand the National Highway (No. 1-A) so that the journey for tourists and passengers may be made more comfortable and mishaps in the *Nashiri* tract may be avoided.

## Air Transport

In a state characterised with mountains, forests and cold desert, development of railways and roads is difficult and expensive. The remote areas of the State of Jammu and Kashmir are not easily accessible. Under such geo-ecological conditions air-transport plays and extremely important role.

The importance of airways increases in the times of emergency like wars, epidemics, famines, devastating floods, snowing and heavy avalanches. The development of airways, however, has been largely constrained by population agglomerations and weather. In particular poor visibility and snowing hinder air-transport in the state.

Both the capitals i.e. Jammu and Srinagar and the Divisional Headquarters of Ladakh (Leh) are on the Air-Map of the country. The Indian Airlines connects the airports of Jammu, Srinagar and Leh. Everyday, there are several flights from Delhi to Srinagar. During the peak tourist season, Delhi-Srinagar remains as one of the most busy air-routes, while on the Jammu-Srinagar route there is heavy rush throughout the year, especially during the winter season, when the National Highway No. 1-A is affected adversely in the Nashiri Land Slide Tract (Batote-Ramban). The Srinagar Jammu cities deserve more flights and especial subsidy to provide more comfort to the people of the state and the tourists.

Though after Independence a spectacular progress has been made in road, railway and air-transport in the state, the situation is still far from satisfactory. Both the road traffic and Indian Airlines are under constant pressure. The transport is quite inadequate to meet the traffic requirements of the people of the state and the tourists coming from the various parts of the country and abroad.

**Table 11.4**
**Jammu & Kashmir State–Goods Exported, 1999-2000**

| Commodity | Quantity |
|---|---|
| 1. Fruits, apples, pears, cherry, others | 43,85,270 qtls. |
| 2. Wood and wood products | 20,43,920 qtls. |
| 3. Gums and resins | 1,75,260 qtls. |
| 4. Metals | 1,62,570 qtls. |
| 5. Dry fruits (almonds, walnut etc.) | 76,100 qtls. |
| 6. Hides and skins etc. | 46,950 qtls. |
| 7. Glass and glass-wares | 29,760 qtls. |

| | | |
|---|---|---|
| 8. | Rubber goods, tyres & tubes | 25,420 qtls. |
| 9. | Turpentine oil | 25,140 qtls. |
| 10. | Fibres | 11,060 qtls. |
| 11. | Cotton and cotton products | 10,990 qtls. |
| 12. | Wool and wool products | 8,890 qtls. |
| 13. | Provisions | 4,590 qtls. |
| 14. | Papier-mache | 1,170 qtls. |
| 15. | Miscellaneous goods* | 18,20,040 qtls. |
| | Total | 88,27,040 qtls. |

*Miscellaneous goods include Anardanas, seeds, bones, drugs, medicines, honey, vegetables, grains, cement, lime, chalk, marble, gypsum, paints, varnish, oilseeds, silk goods, stationery, embroidery goods, cigarettes, tea, fur goods and animals

## Trade

The State of Jammu and Kashmir is essentially an agrarian state in which most of the people are directly or indirectly dependent on forestry, cultivation of crops, sericulture, horticulture and apiculture. Consequently, the state exports a large variety of agro-based and forest based products. Being poor in minerals, imports of machines, chemical products and electric goods is made in the state. The major items exported from the state have been given in Table 11.4.

## Imports

The principal commodities which the state imports include machinery, iron and steel, electric goods, petroleum, fertilizers, chemical elements and compounds, non-ferrous metals, vehicles, petroleum products, paper and paper board, rice, oilseeds, sugar, textile goods, coal-tar, dyes etc. The quantity of the goods imported has been given in Table 11.5.

It may be seen from Table 11.5 that grains, pulses, minerals, petroleum, living animals, cotton goods, iron and steel, vegetables, fodder, coal, electric goods, drugs, milk and milk products, books, sugar, salt, urea and stationery are imported in the state from Punjab, Haryana, Gujarat, Rajasthan, Uttar Pradesh and other parts of the country. It may also be noted from Table 11.5 that the people of the state are largely dependent for a large quantity of essential goods on import from the neighbouring states. The state has been striving consistently for the expansion and diversification of its exports. A series of measures have been put into operation which cover finance for export, assistance and incentives, transport facilities, training, market research and rationalization of institutional arrangements and technical services. Despite many incentives the process of export is slow and most of the goods are exported as raw materials. A pragmatic policy is to be followed to enhance the export processed goods from the state.

**Table 11.5**
**Jammu & Kashmir State–Goods Imported, 1999-2000**

| Commodity | Quantity |
|---|---|
| 1. Grains and pulses | 33,23,310 qtls. |
| 2. Minerals rocks and their products | 24,18,240 qtls. |
| 3. Petrol, diesel, mobil-oil, air trans fuel etc. | 13,66,520 qtls. |
| 4. Living animals (sheep etc.) | 10,82,807 qtls. |
| 5. Cotton and cotton products | 2,08,580 qtls. |
| 6. Iron & iron products | 8,19,370 qtls. |
| 7. Vegetables | 5,49,110 qtls. |
| 8. Fodder | 3,67,800 qtls. |
| 9. Coal and coke | 3,19,930 qtls. |
| 10. Fruits | 2,45,330 qtls. |
| 11. Electric goods | 1,13,120 qtls. |
| 12. Drugs and medicines | 1,11,140 qtls. |
| 13. Leather and its products | 1,06,800 qtls. |
| 14. Provisions, milk powder, butter, ghee, dalda | 3,33,920 qtls. |
| 15. Stationery, books etc. | 1,35,110 qtls. |
| 16. Salt | 1,97,220 qtls. |
| 17. Silk & its products | 1,92,200 qtls. |
| 18. Sugar, molasses and their products | 5,16,780 |
| 19. Oils and their products | 7,29,880 |
| 20. Urea, (NPK) | 4,87,190 |

| 21. Miscellaneous goods* | 26,17,590 |
|---|---|
| Total | 26,15,295 |

*Miscellaneous goods include apparel, crockery, paints and varnishes, fibrous goods, glass and glassware, herber dashry, liquirs, vehicles (2295), motor spare parts, oilseeds, tea, rubber products, wool and its products, soaps, perfumery and cosmetics, hosiery goods, spices, chillies, tobacco products, military load, sports goods, wood and timber, music goods, L.P. Gas etc.

### *References*

1. H.P. White and M.L. Senior, 1983, '*Transport Geography*', Longman, New York.
2. H. Robinson and C.G. Bamford, 1978, '*Geography of transport*', Macdonal & Evans, Playmouth.
3. H.R. Jarrte, 1977, '*A Geography of Manufacturing*', Macdonal and Evans, Playmouth.
4. T.C. Sharma, et.al. 1987, '*Economic and Commercial Geography of India*', Vikas Publ. Co. New Delhi.
5. P.N.K. Bamzai, 1980, '*Kashmir and Central Asia*', Light and Life Publishers, Trivendrum.
6. *National Council of Applied Economic Research*, 1969, Techno-Economic Survey of J & K, New Delhi.

# Bibliography


Agarwal, S.N., 1972, '*India's Population Problems*', Delhi.

Ahmad, M., 1985, '*Spatial Organisation of Tourism in Kashmir State with Especial Reference to Sindh Valley*', Unpublished M. Phil, Dissertation, University of Kashmir.

Aiyer, N.P.K., 1968, '*Field Crops of India*', Bangalore.

Alam, S.M., Dunkerly Joy, et.al., 1985, '*Fuelwood in Urban Markets*', Concept Pub. Co., New Delhi.

*American Encyclopedia of Social Sciences.*

Bali, U.S., 1982, '*Encroachment of Forests in the Jhelum Valley, Kashmir*', Unpublished M.Phil. Dissertation, University of Kashmir.

Bates, C.E., '*A Gazetteer of Kashmir, Jammu*' p. 1.

Bhan, S.N., 1956, '*Snowfall at Srinagar*', Indian Jour. Met. Geo-physics, VII, pp. 295-300.

Bhat, S.A., 1983, '*Regional Structure of Kashmir Division*', Unpublished M.Phil, Dissertation, Kashmir University.

Bose, S.C., 1968, '*Land and People of the Himalayas*', Indian Pub. Calcutta, p. 198.

Buchanan, R.O., 1974, '*An Illustrated Dictionary of Geography*', Mc. Graw Hill, Singapore.

Burrard, S.G., 1933, '*A Sketch of the Geography and Geology of the Himalayas and Tibet*', Pt. III, Delhi.

Chaudhry, M.R., 1970, '*Indian Industries : Development and Location*', Calcutta Census of India, 1971.

*Census of India 1981, Series 8–Jammu and Kashmir, Provisional Population Totals*

Davis, D.H., 1948, '*The Earth of Man*', New York.

*Dept. of Geology & Mining*, Bulletin, 1983

*Digest of Statistics*, Jammu and Kashmir, 1984.

Drew, F., *1971*, '*The Territories of Jammu and Kashmir*', Stanford, Delhi.

Dutta, M., 1985, '*Transport Network Efficiency–A comparative analysis between Jammu and Kashmir Divisions*', Geography of Jammu and Kashmir, edt. M. Husain, Ariana Pub. Co., New Delhi.

Dutta, R.K., and M.G. Gupta, 1967, '*Synoptic Study of the Formation and Movements of the Western Depressions*', Ind. Jour. Met. Geo-physics, XVIII, pp. 45-50.

Flohn, H., 1985, '*Recent Investigation on the Eastern Asia*', Monsoons of the World, IMD, New Delhi.

*Gazetteer of Kashmir and Ladakh*, 1890, Reprinted in 1974 (Vivek, Delhi).

Govt. of India, *Industrial India Annual.*

Govt. of India, *Irrigation and Power Projects,* Ministry of Power and Irrigation, New Delhi, 1970.

Govt. of India, 1970, *Irrigation Atlas of India,* Ministry of Irrigation and Power, New Delhi.

Govt. of Jammu and Kashmir State, *Digest of Statistics*, Srinagar.

Hashia, H., 1988, '*Seasonal Migration of Kashmir Labour*', Rima Publications, New Delhi.

Husain, M., 1994, '*Human Geography*', Rawat Pub. Jaipur.

Husain, M., 1996, '*Systematic Agricultural Geography*', Rawat Pub. Jaipur.

Husain, M., 1994, '*Evolution of Geographical Thought*', Rawat Pub. Jaipur.

Husain, M., 1993, '*Geography of Islamic Countries*', Foundation for Educational Research, New Delhi-25.

Mir, G.M., 1982, '*Impact of Saffron Cultivation on Socio-Economy of the Kashmir Valley*', University of Kashmir, Srinagar.

Husain, M., 1977, '*Human and Economic Geography*', NCERT, New Delhi.

Husain, M., 1979, '*Agricultural Geography*', Inter India Pub. New Delhi.

Husain, M., 1985, '*Major Ethnic Groups of Jammu and Kashmir*', Geography of Jammu and Kashmir, edt. M. Husain, et. al., Ariana Pub. Co. New Delhi.

Husain, M., 2000, '*Systematic Geography of Jammu and Kashmir*' Rawat Publications, Jaipur.

*Imperial Gazetteer of India*, 1908, Vol. XV, London.

*Indian Council of Agricultural Research*, 1970, Handbook of Agriculture, New Delhi.

Jarrett, H.R., 1977, '*A Geography of Manufacturing*', London.

Kachroo, P., '*A Note on Flora of Kashmir*', Geography of Jammu and Kashmir, edt. M. Husain, et.al., New Delhi.

Kanth, T.A., 1985, '*Statigraphic Profile of Jammu and Kashmir*', Geography of Jammu and Kashmir, edt. M. Husain, et.al., New Delhi.

Kendrew, W.G., 1961, '*The Climate of the Continents*', Oxf. Uni. Press, London.

Khatana, R.P., 1985, '*Gujars and Bakarwal Transhumance in Jammu and Kashmir Himalayas : Responses of Spring Migration*', Geography of Jammu and Kashmir, edt. M. Husain, et.al., New Delhi.

Koul, A.K., 1985, '*Home Geography of Jammu and Kashmir*', Srinagar.

Koul, H.N., 1958, '*A Survey of Origin of People of Kashmir*', Kashmir Today, Vol. II, Srinagar.

Koul, M.K., '*Gujjars and Hordes of Jungles*', Kashmir Today, Vol. IV, pp. 7-8.

Koul, V.H. Dar, 1985, '*Changing Vegetation of Kashmir*', Geography of Jammu and Kashmir, edt. M. Husain, et.al., New Delhi.

Kumari, V., 1968, '*The Nilmat Purana*', Vol. I, Jammu, pp. 23-24.

Lawrance, W.R., 1967, '*The Valley of Kashmir*', Srinagar.

Lidhoo, M.L., 1985, '*Gujjar–Their Attitudes Towards Social Changes-Education and Modernization*', Unpublished Project Report, pp. 2-12.

Mam. A. 1984, '*Hanjis of Dal Lake*', Unpublished, M. Phil Dissertation, University of Kashmir, Srinagar.

Monkhouse F.J., et.al., 1973, '*A Dictionary of Natural Environment*, London.

Morgan, et.al., 1973, '*Human and Economic Geography*', London.

Mooley, D.A., 1957, '*The Role of Western Disturbances in the Production of Weather over India during different Seasons*', Ind. Jour. Met. Geo-Physics, VIII, pp. 253-260.

National Council of Applied Economic Research, 1969, '*Techno-Economic Survey of Jammu and Kashmmi*', New Delhi.

Pathik, J., 1980, '*Cultural Heritage of Dogras*', New Delhi.

Plyurnin, '*Reclamative Soil Science*', New Delhi.

Ray, S.C., 1970, '*Early History and Culture of Kashmir*', pp. 26-34.

Raza, M., et.al., 1978, '*The Valley of Kashmir*', Vikas Pub. House, New Delhi.

Raina, A.N., 1971, '*Geography of Jammu and Kashmir*', New Delhi.

Robinson, H., et.al., 1978, '*Geography of Transport*', Macdonald & Evans, Play-mouth.

Rookhrub, L., '*Race and Tribes–Culture of Kashmir*', New Delhi.

Shahi, S.S., '*The Nomads of Himalayas*', Delhi.

Sharma, T.C., O. Coutinho, 1986, '*Economic and Commercial Geography of India*', Vikas Pub. Co., New Delhi.

Stein, M.A., 1976, *Kalhan's Rajtarangani*, p. 386.

Siddique, M., 1986, '*Urbanization in Jammu and Kashmir–A Regional Analysis*', Geography of Jammu & Kashmir, edt. M. Husain, et.al., Ariana Pub. Co., New Delhi.

Sufi, G.M.D., 1979, '*Islamic Culture in Kashmir*', New Delhi.

Symon, L., 1974, '*Agricultural Geography*', London.

Wadia, D.N., 1926, '*Geography of India*', Macmillan, London.

White, H.P. and M.L. Senior, 1983, '*Transport Geography*', London.

Zutshi, B., 1985, '*Population Distribution of Jammu and Kashmir–A Regional Analysis*', Geography of Jammu and Kashmir, edt. M. Husain, et.al., Ariana Publishing Co., New Delhi.

18. Raghunath Temple, Jammu

19. Amar Singh Palace, Jammu

20. Vaishnav Devi, Katra

21. (a) A Kashmiri Beauty, Kashmir

21. (b) Kashmiri Women carrying Breakfast

22. (b) Sowing of Corms by Plough Methods

22. (b) Germinated Corms - ready for Sowing

23. Dishording of Corms

24. Shikaras on hire in Dal Lake

25. Tourism - Pahalgam - Kashmir